Between Pricked Ears

Greg May

A. Brown – Waters Publishers

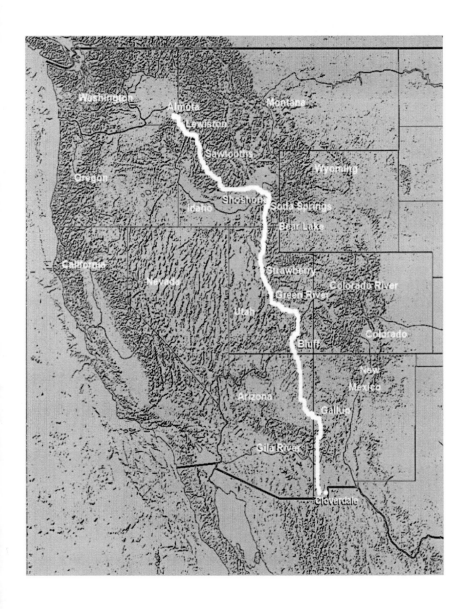

For Maria Julia....

&

In the sincere hopes that this book inspires more humans to never have to say, "I wished I woulda", as their days on this earth reach toward their sunsets...

Author's Notes

On the campus of Bowdoin College in Brunswick, Maine, an Oak tree stands to inspire young minds to persevere and for new graduates to meet and bid their farewells. This tree, known as the Thorndike Oak is a living symbol for this small college, and David Thorndike, a direct descendant of this namesake, was of great assistance both before and during my journey. From the day he poked his 66 year old head into my Wilderness Survival class tipi comprised of college kids, David Thorndike taught me much more than I ever taught him. For David and I, this book is our Oak tree.

I am very grateful for production and editing assistance from Francine Tanguay, Annie's Book Stop in Wells, Maine, Tessa Prest-Berg of Cape Neddick, Maine and Dan Gallagher.

John Knight, the illustrator, and his family truly embraced and supported this project, and the Anchorage-By-The-Sea family in Ogunquit, Maine provided a wonderful environment allowing for its completion. I am forever grateful to both.

ISBN 978-0-615-87480-7

Visit http://asiaislandic.wix.com/greg-may-author for ordering information

Infinite Imaging – York, ME

A. Brown-Waters Publishing Company

Chapters

Prologue

Back in 1996, a man and his horse located the ghost town of Cloverdale, New Mexico, resting on the US-Mexico border. Nestled in a valley between the Chiricahua range to the west, and the Animas range to the immediate east, Cloverdale was a natural rest stop for early settlers, the Apache's of Cochise, and Spanish Conquistadors a few hundred years previous. Satisfied that he had located the first of many ghost towns he had read about in the past, the man turned his horse, stocked with only a canteen, Hudson's Bay blanket, an ancient .32 Winchester rifle, and the weathered buckskins he wore and headed for home, itself the ghost town of Almota, Washington, some 2000 miles to the north.

The following is his story....

1.

2000 Miles To Home

Of all nature's rules, drought is the cruelest.

Near each dirty seep, a hint of a desperate whinny escapes Jelly as he steps out. As desperation eases in to reality, the 2 year old red sorrel Appaloosa- Arabian cross, with white socks and a blaze, again learns a harsh lesson from this land; a dry seep only *smells* like water....

Desert water is a riddle, laughing at those poor souls unable to solve the mystery. In his first two days in the desert, Jelly had already learned to look at riddles with a calm demeanor, despite the escaping whinny born of fear.

Jelly was born on the banks of the Snake River, in southeast Washington State, near the dam that submerged the ghost town of Almota and provided the State of Idaho with a seaport. The Nez Perce and Palouse Indians ran their thousands of horses on these 'Breaks', known due to the cascading basalt outcroppings descending from 2000' to 600' in a quarter mile range. A perfect environ for horses, not so much for humans. Moisture, water and feed are available year round despite 100 degree summer temperatures in the narrow canyons. The 'Breaks' were the only land Jelly had known, a land where water could be found at a number of year round springs, despite having to work hard to get to them.

The basalt cliffs were great teachers, and prepared him well for the deserts. He learned the ways of the rattlesnake, cougar and scorpion in his first six months of life.

This was his first venture into the high deserts in the southwest, and the month of March was just beginning to allow its sparse grasses to emerge. Still, the fear of learning that water is not always where you sniff it, created a great deal of stress in the young horse.

At well over 15 hands tall and already well muscled for an Arabian-Appaloosa cross, the flat rocky terrain posed no problems for the horse. Strange smelling prickly plants and weird looking critters occupied his wide open eyes and his continually perked ears. Jelly knew he was in for the ride of his life....

-2-

Rider

Rider could never be a politician, banker or lawyer, though the last profession he had had a go at. Failed miserably did he. Wasn't blessed with a tolerance for bullshit; never did, never would. He had all the people skills of a troll. In his late thirties, balded by razor and choice, with a set of grey eyes of a smiling wolf, he knew his best days of physical strength were still within sight on his back trail, but the bridge in that direction disappeared, and he wasn't in the mood to rebuild it. He knew he'd never see that trail again, and he wondered if it was vanity the led him to this unforgiving desert run amuck with drug and people smugglers. A lone horseman is an inviting target. Arthritis was already surrounding the broken bones of a rough n' tumble early manhood. Inwardly he felt himself a coward for not being tough enough to change his intake or lifestyle, preferring to tolerate the pain and lost vanity with more whiskey than was necessary. He had a biting wit when he chose to visit humans, but that wasn't often. He always preferred dogs and animals rather than children, adult or otherwise. He carved out a life on the harsh basalt cliffs that guided the Snake River through the southeast corner of the State of Washington, a day's ride from the Idaho line. Most folk weren't sure what to make of him, but they knew that in an emergency, it wasn't in him to fail a task or decline to aid another.
Those folks who had the cajones to hike the half mile

rattlesnake filled climb to his barn and tipi predicted that there would still be talk about him fifty years after he was gone. There was no place in his fiber for a God, his early years as an orphan and an acquired set of parents that preferred nightly drug fueled beatings had seen to that. Without a family or a deity to hold him, he was gone by his eighteenth birthday, visited back a few times, but was gone nonetheless.

He returned in later life to guide the parents to the other side, for there was no one else and it was the right thing to do. He had his share of women but was never capable or tough enough to hold even the few he had truly loved. He couldn't bear to be touched when asleep, and never could escape the childhood beatings in his mind, so he stopped trying. He was a hair under 6' tall, not particularly fast or strong. What he lacked in muscle he made up for in a bullheaded mindset that wasn't capable of quitting. He knew that someday this trait would get him dead- he wasn't ever going to die in his sleep. As a boy he was never far from the sea, and all that went with that life, but when he had ventured west a decade previous, the smell of horseshit trumped that of seaweed.

Jelly got his name from a mis-pronunciation of Jerry, the toughest SOB he had ever met. Jerry was a wiry gent borne out of the Oregon logging camps a decade or two Rider's senior, and a cow professor at a somewhat nearby university to the Snake. Jerry had a grad student from China, who spoke English as best he could, and when Jelly was rejected by his momma at birth, Rider could only reach the grad student. While trying to find Jerry for assistance, the communicated message named the foal even before the first forced suckle. Jerry was pronounced as *Jelly*.

Jerry was the real deal and Rider remora'd himself to being more of a pain-in-the-ass than the 'fessor should have tolerated, but he couldn't seem to be able to shuck Rider. Such as it was. All that Rider had learned about horses, forthrightness and bone numbing hard work leaked from the professor and his close circle.

Real western men were like that, and Rider wanted to be that.

Rider was content to be a lone wolf on the cliffs high above the Snake River where modern conveniences didn't reach, and he did not want them anyway. He was too busy reading any and all treatise about mountain men, Indians, cowboys and most importantly ghost towns, since he lived near one. One day he decided that he had just about enough reading, so it was time to find the ghost towns of yore. And off he went.

-3-

That First step

Skirting Old Mexico near the ghost town of Cloverdale, New Mexico, Rider set his eyes north toward home on the Snake River, 2000 miles away. Turning Jelly, Rider rested in his saddle, scanned the northern skyline, peering between pricked ears.

With the Animas Mountains five miles to the east, just inside of the New Mexico-Arizona-Old Mexico border, the Chiricahua Mountain Range a couple miles to the west, Jelly set a comfortable stroll northward. Animas Peak tops out at 8500' and boasts its very own species of rattlesnake. Knowing this from chatting with the only passerby he would see all day, Rider had already decided to bed down that evening on the western slope! The Chiricahuas were home to the last stronghold for Cochise in the late 1800's. The Apache leader controlled the region for two decades until his murder while under US Army guard. So impenetrable were these mountains that the few available accesses into the range were exposed, and could be defended by few sentinels. Eyesight reaches farther than bullets, and any thought of gaining advantage in these hills via surprise attack was functionally mute. Cochise people, (native clans were often known by their leaders names), lived quite peacefully in these hills knowing that the creator of such built a natural fortress far better than any man ever could. Every water hole for hundreds of miles was known, maintained and protected. In battle or attack, the Apache's most effective bullet was patience, since once escape routes were hobbled, time was their most effective weapon. None of their enemies could ever outrun thirst.

The valley between the ranges is harsh desert. Water 'might' be found at scarce seeps, shaded arroyos, or at stock tanks fed by windmills. The riddle is discerning from a distance which choice is the most likely to hold drinkable water; for a thirsty horse and rider is a horse and rider in grave trouble. The greatest survival skill in the desert is not the ability to find water, but the ability not to be without water. Approaching windmills simply because they were there soon proved to be folly, as a rancher manages his range by keeping tanks filled or empty by disconnecting the drive line to the pump. The windmill still spins, but does not pump water. By disconnecting the drive line, the rancher is able to rotate his stock animals to other pastures where the drive line is connected, assuring that only a particular stock tank is full of water. By grazing his range in this manner, non-stock animals also alter their life circle to follow the water, creating potential conflict. Ranchers generally not only disconnected but also removed the pump drive lines. Even having never seen a desert before, Rider had enough common sense to know that when water sources are rare, cattle tanks also serve desert critters. The scarcer the water, the farther away from that water Rider sleeps. The only way Rider could find out if a tank held water was to ride close and look inside. The abundance or freshness of tracks also helped, but by the time enough tracks were found, he was almost to the tanks anyway.

Windmills are usually about 5 miles apart, and checking each one can mean a lot of extra riding for no benefit, and great risk of dehydration for both man and beast. Extra saddle time in the desert places one at needless risk, so the Rider had to think of

12

a different approach. The obvious approach was to track the movement of the animals, herd and hunter. Tracking takes time, and Rider was traveling through, not traveling around. He wanted to get gone.

-4-

Movin' on

Desert sand is a notorious holder of sign, one tracks by shape rather than definition. This renders the skill of 'ageing' sign beyond 48 hours old a difficult chore, even in consistent weather conditions. The desert is the epitome of consistent. Often more is learned by clues outside the track rather than what is inside. Each track is a chapter and a trail of tracks is the novel. Rider was constantly judging whether to track or travel, a life determining balance. Too much tracking for water can sap the body's reserves, increasing the pressure of the pursuit. Instinct fortified by knowledge, skill and unerring focus determines life and death when traveling in harsh environs. A desert track 'rolls its edges' as if it were a cynical jester smirking from the ground. A two day old track reveals little difference from one that is five days old. There is a much greater likelihood that a recent trail of tracks heads to water than does an older set. Hunting water in the desert is more an exercise of preservation and patience than of skill and cunning. Rider chose the time of day to move, avoiding the hot, and traveling in the cool. Lush green grass means water and dull green grass means long roots and a lot of digging. Seeps are mostly found on the sheltered, westerly facing, leeward cut banks of arroyos. Unfortunately, these are also good locations for quicksand. Rider also avoided traveling too far away from the foothills, as the likelihood of shade and water is greater in hilly terrain versus the flat desert. Like all environs, the desert has its own flow and buzz.

A lone horseman is vulnerable to many dangers; primary among these is other people. A hundred years ago a rider assumed anyone met on the trail was an enemy until proven otherwise. Today, the land is governed by laws that demand a lone horseman must assume anyone met on the trail is a friend until proven otherwise. The risk of this kind of proof is risk itself.

Rider kept his camps out of sight lines and a fair distance from where Jelly was hobbled, recognizing that Jelly might be too attractive a quarry to pass up for some. Rider wanted to sleep hidden where he could see but not be seen. Even if someone found Jelly munching on whatever might be available, it would be difficult to spot a sleeping soul.

Supper on the trail was just before dusk and usually consisted of hare, rattlesnake, dried meat or fish prepared over a quick, hot, smokeless fire, in a small pit. Fuel was gathered from the ground, no cutting of branches or trees revealing evidence of his passing, or loud noises of his presence in the silent desert. The supper routine lacked any mention of a God, but was religious in essence. After supper, Jelly and Rider moved on for another hour or so and chose a sleep spot for both. Rider never wanted to sleep where he cooked or ate; too many attractive smells for critters to pass-up. Jelly learned to poop at supper, and Rider made good use of it in camouflaging the smells or campfire evidence. The entire supper process of fuel gathering, cooking, eating, clean-up and evidence removal took no more than 30 minutes. Jelly enjoyed the after supper strolls, walking along side Rider like a young son heading to the baseball field with his Dad- in the Norman Rockwell sense. He knew the day was done.

Approaching a potential campsite was done with great care. First Rider would scan the sight lines to see from which direction he might be vulnerable from any humans that might stumble upon his camp. At best, adequate feed and water for Jelly within a small area was sought, or access to it. In '96, the southwestern United States was in the midst of a severe drought that had a devastating effect on the range. Rider did not know this before he started for home; he kinda walked into it. Grass was available only in pockets, dead cattle littered the land. The coyotes, javelina and vultures flourished.

With water being so scarce, Rider made sure to keep his camps a good distance from it. Knowing that all critters would come to water sometime, he didn't want to be in conflict with any or all. When investigating a possible campsite, he would walk the perimeter, examining the ground for recent predator, snake or mouse sign. If fresh predator sign was found, he would simply move on, away from their life circle. If snake trail was found, it would be followed to its maker, or a safe distance away. All mouse holes within 30' radius of his bed would be filled in, as these underground railways can be home to scorpions, black widows and various snakes; critters Rider did not wish to sleep with. Lounging around a campfire as depicted in western movies was the stupidest thing Rider could imagine. He knew that in times before, that practice meant certain death by another's hand. The attraction of humans was not a circumstance he wanted to afford. A bad guy sighting or approaching a campfire has a great advantage. He can see in, you can't see out. Rider was content to fold himself into his Hudson Bay blanket, designed so no critters could enter from below and share body heat. Not fool proof, but better than relying on a coil of horsehair rope allayed on the ground-another fallacy from the western movie genre. Rattlesnakes aren't bothered by horsehair at all-not one bit. If truth be told, mice like to chew on the sweat soaked fibers, and everybody knows what eats mice....

With the sleep site selected, Rider would slide the gear off of Jelly and tie the halter rope around Jelly's foreleg and let him graze. The 'whip rope' made it uncomfortable should Jelly decide to run, as the rope would whip him like a snake as he ran. Horses quickly learn that no matter how far or fast they run, they can't outrun that nasty 'snake'! It's an old-timers trick certainly shunned today, mostly due to the ignorance of actual life-on-the-trail 'horsemen'. Part of the trick is to only do it to a tired horse that has been 'snaked' before-hobbles then don't seem so bad! As Rider set to the task of constructing his bed from the saddle pad,

Hudson Bay blanket and saddle, Jelly would contently chomp away at whatever was in reach.

Prior to the sun setting, a stick was tapped in the ground so its shadow could be traced. By knowing the path of the shadow, Rider was able to determine north and consequently the following day's direction. Once the sleep nest was finished Rider picked up his rifle and wandered to some high point to scan north, setting any landmarks and likely watering stops to memory for the next day. In the waning light the back trail was scanned until he could no longer see. In the hour it took to complete these tasks, which Rider did religiously each night, Jelly had cooled off sufficiently to allow for an effective rubdown. Rider gathered a few bundles of dried grass and rubbed it against the horse's hair, wicking as much moisture out of his skin and hair as possible. Leaving the hair standing on end allowed for better air drying and a decreased chance for sores, or hot spots to take hold. Jelly's feet were cleaned out, inspected for stones or sores, and rubbed with Prickly Pear Cactus juice Rider had prepared. Removing the whip rope, Jelly was either tethered so he could graze in a circle, or hobbled if the terrain was rugged, as a hobbled horse is not as likely to wander in rugged terrain as he might on flatter land.

On the first night, Jelly slept little. Every noise was one he never heard up on his home above the Snake River. Every shadow was a monster. The grass Rider collected for him smelled funny and tasted weird. The air was thicker and sweeter. The water was awful and the stars were plentiful. His dried sweat made him feel heavy. No clouds anywhere at all and he knew that no rain was near-he couldn't even smell a hint. Little did he know that it would be 73 days before he felt a drop.

5

JT

JT did not have a nose.

He had a strap and mask across what was left of his face to guard against dust, where his nose once was. In his 80's, he still worked his small ranch, even after cancer from the copper mines stole his face. Standing a few inches above 6' tall, it seemed his ribs showed through his shirt, much like the horses and cattle in this drought stricken land. He had lived around Animas, New Mexico all his life and had no intention of going anywhere else, even when he had his face.

It had only been 3 days since Jelly discovered the desert, and his stress was taking more weight off him than the 60 miles he and Rider had covered. The first afternoon Jelly found himself in the middle of 20 wild horses, biting and kicking at him, while Rider slashed at the attackers with his mecate, or lead rope, finally outrunning them. After a mile the attackers tired of getting their eyes whipped by the weird smelling buckskin clad man astride an obviously terrified young horse. Jelly had almost maxed out his allotment of fear and was uncontrollably letting out small whinnies hoping Zadie, his middle-aged Momma, might magically appear. These small broods of wiry, mean horses were in ravaged condition, full of oozing cuts and sores, pounced upon Jelly in a heartbeat without a sound. A sight to behold they were and the farther off they ran, the better they looked to both horse and rider.

Under the sentinel gaze of the 8500' Animas Peak, Jelly was first turned south to scout for the storied ghost town of Cloverdale, and to touch the sand of the Mexican-American border. People did not live in these remote parts because it was drop dead inhospitable. The border was a rusted 3-wire barbed wire fence, more of it cut down than standing up.

Cloverdale sits on the border, and about 200 souls enjoyed the constant back-and-forth cross border cattle and horse raiding around 1900. In the late 1880's the Apache band of Chief Loco, (the true source of where the term 'loco' comes from), killed about 40 settlers in the area and skirmishes lasted for another couple decades before even the heartiest souls either died or gave up. By the 1920's all that remained was a building that was once the southernmost Post Office in the State and a forgotten cemetery. The building remains today, keeping hay out of the sun.

Three days of alternating riding and walking found the pair in the one store town of Animas just at dusk. Rider wandered into the small store and bought a Coke and some ham. While inside, Rider watched as JT stopped his pickup and looked over the horse, then turned around and drove off. Rider thought nothing of it. He led Jelly across the dirt road to a lean-to and small coral, stripped the gear, and turned Jelly loose. The cowshit in the corral was as hard as cement, and Jelly was rolling around before Rider dropped his saddle under cover. Rider filled up the small water trough from an ancient spigot, and set about organizing a bed for the night nearby. By the time Jelly had drunk his fill, JT returned, spotted Jelly, and dropped off a half a bale of alfalfa, and drove off, having never said a word the entire time.

Rider rose to howdy, but JT wouldn't have it, so Rider cracked his Coke and hunkered down atop the cowshit. Both thirsts quenched, Rider set about inspecting the fence of the small corral, tossing out strands of barbed wire that highway workers had tossed in. With the drought, corrals were empty and cattle weren't worth a penny, and hadn't been for some time. So Jelly had hit the jackpot, great feed, clear, fresh pumped water, safe sleeping within a corral. Rider settled upon his saddle pad and blanket, softened by the two foot thick bed of dried cowshit, and savored a granola bar for supper.

JT returned the next morning with another flake or two of alfalfa. Hay was up to $12 a bale in the drought, and he refused payment. As Jelly was getting a good rubdown, JT leaned against the shed and took the opportunity to speak to someone other than himself in an obvious long while, and was quite surprised and pleased that Rider looked him in the eye as they began to chat.

JT had grown weary of people convulsing in puke spasms at the first site of the remaining part of his face; Rider never gave it a thought, and JT relaxed. One fella talking to another; simple as that. After years of being shunned, JT had sought solace in loneliness and critters. Rider figured there was a parable in that thought somewhere, for his comfort shared a connection with critters also.

JT talked to Rider confining his gaze to Jelly, holding to his learned habit of keeping his face out of direct view. Cancer from the Phelps-Dodge mines set store in his sinuses that once discovered, far too late, correlated with the cancer of his pension that went bankrupt with the copper mine he had given his life and two wives to. The series of operations on his face had bled not only his savings, but also his pride of being something of a ladies' man back in his prime. The first wife died of God knows what, and the second wife left soon after his face did. Taking a shot at setting the old man at ease, and being unafraid of sharing a good giggle, Rider asked him if his self-proclaimed prowess with the ladies was more of a cause for his bachelorhood than his facial features. Their eyes held and it was clear that JT could detect a hint of a smirk on Rider's face, and Rider could detect the same on JT's lips, even though he didn't have any. With a squinted glint in his eye and a relief that this stranger had just treated him simply as a guy, just a normal guy, JT retorted asking Rider if he was born an asshole or was it something he went to school for? Rider, without missing a breath replied that being an asshole was simply an acquired skill, draped his arm around JT's shoulder and gave the old cowboy a quick squeeze as tears welled up in JT's eyes.

Life long friends were made then and there in about a 10 minutes time, and JT looked Rider directly in the eyes when speaking, from that point forward. JT spent the next 20 minutes lecturing Rider about all the potential dangers each sunrise would bring as he scratched his way north in an effort to dissuade Rider from continuing his journey and instead consider moving on to JT's place for a while and helping him fix his place up for a spell. JT knew the answer before he spoke the words, but he had to try. Rider simply told him that it was bad timing, appreciated the offer, but needed to eat miles before the impending summer caught him in the sun baked lowlands of southern Idaho/Montana. JT understood.

It was in JT's eyes that Rider first detected what he would see in the eyes of most of the people he would cross trails with in the coming months. Meeting Rider, these people would see their unfulfilled fantasies and dreams that would never be more powerful than their fears. Many would say how they wished they could come along or try such a journey themselves. They wanted to touch Rider as if 'counting coup' on the type of spirit that is stronger than fear, all in hopes that some of that spirit would transfer to their own soul, though knowing it never would. As by nature Rider recognized and respected their turmoil and remained quiet, encouraging and polite. He learned long ago that true strength is not born in another.

Just shy of dark both Rider and JT knew that both had chores to do. A quick solid handshake married to a quick "so-long" defied the emotions both knew were dancing on their skin, but neither was allowed to release, because that is not what backcountry guys do.   As JT reached his pickup, he spoke to the emerging stars and said that all in all, it was a hell of a ride that he knew was coming to an end.   That gave him comfort.

As he bade farewell, to the horse mostly, he suggested that Rider should keep near the road to Lordsburg, 40 miles north. United States Customs Officers, Border Patrol and 'Coyotes', would likely disrupt Rider's travels if discovered. 'Coyotes' was the term used for slave traders near the border, smuggling 'wets' into the US- 'wet' being people from south of the border trying to get into the US for work. The worst of this 'Coyote' lot were downright cruel, taking money from all who were desperate enough to take a chance at finding work in the US, then 'disposing' of those who did not fill their quota. Young women and girls never got 'disposed' of by this crowd. Rider had heard enough about these modern day comancheros to adjust to riding by moonlight and sleep during the day. JT said he would not have considered that, but allowed that Rider would probably outsmart the lot of them anyway and pitied the poor bastards dumb enough to get in his way.

6

Sleep

For six years, Rider had lived in the Northwest Mountains, trying to track down big-footed animals that weren't really there. He would winter near Washington State University, reviewing the past year's discoveries, and planning and calculating the next spring's adventures for an anthropologist who taught there. Rider fed himself by teaching and lecturing to others across the country about the flourishing in mountain environments.

These years of mountain living provided for his mastery of a number of skills. He became an intuitive animal trailer, guided by observation and delicate patience. The most challenging aspect of living in the hills was the acquired art of learning how to sleep in a survival situation. All survival skills are important and interconnected, but Rider had learned that tired people make life threatening mistakes. After unsaddling Jelly, Rider would dry the pad and blanket over a bush or a limb. With desert temperatures dipping below freezing at night, sleeping warm in his 6-point Hudson Bay blanket required a little effort.

The Hudson Bay Company had entered the beaver fur industry in the early 1700's in Canada and soon became a major player in western expansion in the US also. The management of the company controlled not only the highly lucrative fur market, but were the first private military dealers, as we now know them in recorded history, though not an advertised claim at the time. Whiskey was also a lucrative aspect of their business portfolio and their best kept dirty little secret. Instead of frontal attack, they innocently supplied the enemy with a few barrels of whiskey and strolled in enemy camps amidst the groans and vomit that only a well earned hangover can instill. They controlled the market by controlling people; brokering deals with Indian Tribes, land owners, military brass and the like. Sans standard currency the methods of trade was barter, and nobody did it better than the Hudson Bay Company, or the HBC as it was commonly referred to. Beaver pelts, or plews, were graded and collected at the frontier trading posts and bundled into 'packs' in preparation of shipments back to England where 'fur' hats were the European status symbol of the day. Other than whiskey, gunpowder, and arms the Hudson's Bay blankets were the pricier and more sought after wares. The size of the blanket was defined by 'points', as signified by a dark erect penis length line woven into the side of the blanket. And yes, that is how the length of the line was originally determined. A 3-point blanket was valued at 3 prime beaver pelts for example. A 6-point blanket was a much larger blanket, but also cost more pelts. The post traders were notoriously crooked and seemingly disorganized but that was a calculated ruse. Frontier posts had a well organized communication system and one of the more seemingly devious mechanisms the 'company' employed to control the burgeoning frontier was to manipulate the price structure among differing customer tribes. Blankets came in different colors, and traders all along the frontier could recognize different tribes because they would only trade a certain color to a certain tribe, and thereby each tribe had its own color and accorded price structure. In this manner HBC could create conflicts among the tribes thus assuring constant bickering and little chance of them organizing a single band of natives too large and dangerous to control. T'was an ingenious plan with a fatal flaw.

In their efforts to keep the frontier divided, HBC never expected that tribes would trade amongst themselves, and during trade, the price manipulations were soon exposed. The result was that in their sacrosanct efforts to keep the tribes divided, they produced the opposite result once the manipulation was discovered. Hatred for HBC became prevalent and too dangerous for outlying trading posts and the 'factors' or managers of same. The retreating HBC provided an environment for upstart independent fur companies to compete, and it was these bands of mountain men that truly 'opened' the western lands on the continent and thereby secured the future sovereignty for a soon-to-be self-ruled Canada and United States of America.

While the 6-point blanket was adequate for Rider, the dried saddle pad on top of a matting of collected grasses provided a bed of insulation from the heat sapping frozen ground. Crumbled wild sage was tossed in the nest to ward off the bugs n' such. All the natural materials used for insulation was dead material for, if it were green, the body heat mixed with the drying grass resulted in a moist, clammy, and unnecessary wakeup call at the coldest time of the desert night.

Not being able to sleep when one wants to is more damaging then not getting any sleep at all. Sleep deprived and frustrated people eventually make bad choices, which in nature, is highly risky. Sleeping 'still' takes practice when sleeping 'in' a natural material bed. The more shifting during the night, the more insulation gets flattened and dispersed, and hence, the colder the body becomes. Reconstructing a nest after midnight is not only uncomfortable and loud, but disrupts the sleep routine. A poorly constructed nest may lead to a sequence of results for that sloppiness, which in turn may end in injury or death due to the lack of rest. Rider knew this and made his beds with great care. While this concept may seem paranoid to the gortex-wearing, city-dwelling, environmental naturalist crowd, there is documented evidence detailing the importance of adequate sleep in survival situations. Rescued hikers and climbers world-wide invariably mention how the lack of sleep led to their predicament. Stories of warriors making their way back from enemy lands only to be captured a short distance from friendly lines, abound. Tired, hungry and sleep deprived, their decisions became impaired, and consequently, more careless than if they had a good sleep. As with all wilderness skills, not having the training to sleep well has consequences, though often not immediate.

Settling in his nest for the evening, Rider allowed his ears to become acquainted with the night sounds. Each night has a rhythm or a cadence to which the ears and brain can adjust. Years of sleeping in the wilds trained Rider's brain for the ability to differentiate between noises within this rhythm from those outside of same. Sleeping sound and sleeping light are not mutually exclusive terms. A pigging string was tied from his finger to his canteen, as critters can smell water, and the canteen the most likely article to be nudged. Pigging strings were long, narrow strips of leather attached to a saddle used to tie gear to it. His rifle chamber lay under his right hand under the blanket, assuring it would not get wet or freeze. To be awakened by a noise in the wilderness is simply a case of self preservation. How that noise is reacted to determines said preservation. One learns to awaken with his eyes only, not giving the slightest indication that he/she is awake. The course of action, if any, is then determined by the circumstances. If a bed site is well selected, it melds into the landscape, seemingly protected from approach on one side. An awakened nester is confident realizing that the field of view can be scanned with the eyes without moving and knowing that behind him is safe territory. A good bed site might sit just inside some vegetation or an area of transition from one type of vegetation to another. The selected site allows the nester to monitor various fields of view while remaining concealed. Rider felt most at ease with his head propped against a boulder, hillside or tree, while his eyes faced east, allowing for the warming sunrise alarm clock. He knew just how much water to drink as he had filled his kidneys to the level where pee time correlated with the first streaks of dawn. Storm systems generally come from the west, so his nest faced away from the prevailing winds that can shoot right through the nest and chill the bones. His saddle was a windbreak, not a pillow as Hollywood western movies had concocted. Keeping the saddle upright also allowed the fleece underside to dry from the sweat of the horse. When waking time comes, only the eyelids move and the ears are turned up to maximum volume. Sudden moves can be deadly, as would be proven to Rider in the weeks to come. If he hadn't the discipline to awake in a controlled manner with a Black Widow spider crawling up his arm while sleeping in the Apache nation, and waking up in the company of 2 rattlesnakes in Utah, Rider would likely have attended his own wake.

7.

Heat

There was no wind in New Mexico the morning Rider left Animas just before dawn. After four hours in the saddle the mid-day heat was getting an early start. By mid-morning Rider was already scanning for shelter to hole up till the sun burned itself out about mid-afternoon. In the desert, traveling fast is traveling stupid. The best way to conserve water is to avoid being thirsty, so given that the evening moon would be bright enough to see by, Rider had already decided to keep moving that night. This close to the border bad boys and with no maps or trails, night time travel also afforded him some stealth.

A little copse of scraggly trees in a shallow arroyo brought some welcome shady relief to both beast and man. After staking Jelly and removing his saddle, Rider whipped up a framework of sticks and slung his blanket over the top to wait out the sun in the cooler shade. Having collected a couple armfuls of grass for Jelly from the unreachable edges of the wash, Rider dug a 2' deep hole and watched the water slowly seep in. Between snoozes Rider would grab some more grass, deepen the seep hole he had dug in the sand, and watched as Jelly never let the water within get more than a few inches deep.

Nothing moved.

By 4pm the worst of the sun had relented enough to allow a steady slight breeze to filter into the landscape, still shimmering with waves of heat.

After cleaning Jelly's unshod feet and rubbing a bit of prickly pear cactus juice on Jelly's sunburned nose, Rider led Jelly up and out of the arroyo. Rider enjoyed walking along side his horse probably more than sitting atop. Still recovering from a broken vertebra between his shoulder blades, and the resulting lingering pain in his legs, walking in buffalo hide moccasins on desert sand was good therapy. A few months back Jelly was learning that Rider would sometimes be sitting on his back and would steer him with his legs and tightness around his nose because of a Mexican bosal, rather than a piece of steel in his mouth, as most did. Vaquero's fashioned bosals out of rope or rawhide as a mechanism to steer a horse. A loop fit over the nose of a horse and was connected to the reins and also a lead rope, or a mecate. The loop over the nose would create a raw spot that the horse would eventually shy away from the discomfort, and in this manner the horse learned to turn away from the pain, and that is how the vaquero taught his horse to turn. By the time the raw spot healed, the horse was well trained to move away from that pressure. One windy afternoon during this learning process, an errant plastic bag and a buzzing rattlesnake sent the young horse into such a tizzy that he tried to climb a black walnut tree. His hooves didn't grip as he had hoped and he fell backwards landing on Rider. It hurt, but they remained pals. As dusk approached Rider scanned the northern horizon and waited to marry the last visions of landscape with corresponding stars. When the North Star appeared he drew an arrow in the sand and peered through the vagueness for landmarks, lining up those ahead and behind and set off. Since leaving Animus they had traveled about 12 miles, and Rider hoped to make another 15 through the night. He figured they had another 80 miles to go before they reached the Gila River; at least that was what JT had figured. The Gila River meant good grass, clean water and a well earned bath for Jelly and him. They had one town and one highway to cross, and Rider wanted to get through both in the middle of the night, drawing little or no attention. Shortly after the crescent moon appeared, Jelly kicked his first rusty can. The desert was light enough at 2am so Rider could forget about his point star and navigate by keeping himself in the valley between the shapes of the mountains. A few more rusty cans, a broken cast iron skillet and the remnants of an ancient wooden wagon wheel brought Jelly and Rider to a stop. Dismounting, Rider walked in front of Jelly along a wide shallow swale in the sand. The strewn cans and bottles were old, at least a 100 years was his guess. Shapes appeared silhouetted against the night sky like petrified sentinels. Rider placed his hand over Jelly's muzzle and waited. Light being tricky when not fully alive, Rider still could not determine what it was he was looking at.

Being well trained in the art of remaining patiently still, Rider knew that whatever was out there would move first. Rider used the forgotten skill of focusing on an object by looking beyond it. With ears pricked and eyes wide, Rider's comforting hand thwarted Jelly's instinct to bolt. It was this gentle hand that Jelly had learned to trust since his first breath in Rider's arms. Jelly's momma had rejected the foal at first and at 22 years old, would not survive the following winter. Zadie, his momma, only tolerated the little horse because he brought relief to full udder of milk. Had the old mare ever figured out a different method of relief other than her foal, she likely would have stomped the little horse to death upon his first attempt to suckle. It was in this seeming rejection that the foal found more comfort in the funny smelling, two-legged critter, with the gentle hand.

The desert became loud with silence as bits of light began to bring morning closer to day. The horse and rider continued to remain stock-still scrutinizing the silent shapes emerging in the distance. Finally, Rider convinced himself that he had out- waited any potential living creature, and stepped forward with Jelly on a short tether. With the mecate (the 3rd rein of a bosal), held short, a horse cannot gain much momentum to jump should a spook be too much for the horse brain to handle. Moving closer, the distant sentinels evolved into remnants of old sandstone posts and walls, supporting sky where roofs once stood.

It all made sense now. The spirits of the long since passed remained in this place, and Rider knew he had stumbled into another ghost town.

-8-
Shakespeare

Shakespeare was a 'wild west' town in the truest sense back in the 1850's. It was a lawless and short-lived boom to bust town, as most ghostowns of the Old West were. When silver was being hauled out of the nearby mountains the town had a booming population of more than 3000 souls. The town enjoyed widespread notoriety for swift justice or rather swift hangings, 'justice' often being a niggling factor in the equation. The Campo Santo cemetery outside of town is still visible and testament to said 'justice'. Shakespeare was graced by some of the more noted personalities of the Old West such as Billy-the-Kid, John Slaughter and the like. The Butterfield Stage Company had constructed a solid adobe station in the town, complete with stout log beams hauled from the distant mountains. These beams not only held up the roof, but also served as the gallows of justice since mesquite bushes weren't tall or tough enough to hold the dead weight of a man. In addition to occasional hanging events, the station also had a café where the house 'rules' were known far and wide. No food would be served until the hanged bodies, including their last soilings, were removed from the premises. By the late 1800's Shakespeare had fallen into disrepair and the weathering remnants were what Rider was strolling through as the sun began to waken. With no cover in sight for miles, Rider devoted little time to wondering about the layout of the town, in favor of getting to some semblance of shade and water up the invisible trail north. In the desert the sun can transform from life giver to life taker in an instant. Tightening the cinch, Jelly moved out at a steady trot in hopes of seeing something, anything, that wasn't flat arid desert. Jelly was homesick for green grass, a few trees and his buddies back on the Snake River range. The horse did not like his situation-not at all. Rider knew the young horse was struggling mentally but tried to keep him focused at the task at hand. He dismounted and talked to the young horse while stroking Jelly's neck. After ten minutes of gentle parenting he mounted and moved out at a forced walk, purposefully keeping Jelly walking in a straight line. Rider figured he had 4-5 hours of travel time before he and Jelly would be at the mercy of the life giving sun's alter ego.

-9-

Quint

At 5'6' Quint Cabarga was a compact pistol, so Rider gave him one.

A month previous, Quint had received the stranger and his young sorrel horse as a stout well trained horse receives a cue. Rider had brought along a palm .22 caliber Colt to use as his hideout gun. He figured the old fella could use it now more than Rider would need it. Quint had grown fearful of tending to his horses out back in his sheds due to the increasing regularity of uninvited 'guests' from Old Mexico. Quint doubted that he could ever use the gun to kill another but the reassurance of packing that small piece of iron, as well as knowing who had given it to him, made him feel a little taller. Rider had told him to carry the 'pocket confidence' out to the sheds when doing his chores. He was always trailed by his wild cow mutt, Brandy, and his tiny wiener dog, Muffin, neither of whom inspired much protective confidence.

Like Quint, his Last Penny Ranch was clinging on to a thread of life when Rider unexpectedly entered both gates one early spring afternoon. With the south fence of the ranch being a dry spit from the international line in the sand between the USA and Mexico, the Last Penny was often home to more transient 'wets' than Quints remaining horses. seventy years old and alone, Quint had the capacity to exhibit kindness, fairness and devout conduct interspersed with a miraculously quick anger that only a true Spanish 'jefe' in the Gothic sense could muster in a snap.

Modern medicine had provided a 'miracle' on Quint's cancerous throat a few years back, similar to how it had transformed JT's face back in Animas. Both JT and Quint had worked in the same mine but never knew each other. Quint had worked 30 years in that mine and it butchered his throat as well as his promised pension. While JT's sorrow was his loss of pride fortified by lust from the opposite sex, Quint's woe, was in his mind, a loss of honor. This perceived loss was confirmed and reflected in his beloved horses shying away from the electrically charged monotone that now resonated from the little microphone he had to press against his throat in order to be heard. No longer able to use both of his hands on his horses because he had to hold the little gizmo with one, he couldn't feel their emotions while training. The little gizmo did not allow him to whisper to the critters he had built his life and self-worth around, and as his heart waned, he found his life shying away just as his horses did now. While the interior of his stucco hacienda was impeccably maintained, the defeated condition of the corrals, pens, and sheds seemed to reflect his inner sorrow. Quint was fighting off the unrelenting sand that continually entered the two bit hole the doctors had cut out in the front of his throat to access the cancerous parts as desperately as he sorrowed over the sand that was slowly swallowing his ranch, knowing he couldn't really do anything about either.

Each morning he woke and waited until there was enough light to see, and then wandered out back to feed his horses which, much to his dismay, he kept penned up. He feared that they would easily free themselves from the 6 acre pasture whose fences were no match for the onslaught of the 'wets' and the weather, and if that happened, his perceived self worth as a horseman would take yet another hit . He was running out of hits.

In the days that Rider stayed on the Last Penny so Jelly could acclimate himself to the desert, Quint spent his time with Jelly and Rider spent his time fixing fence. It was a good trade, though Quint's time with the young Jelly was far more valuable. Quint ground-trained Jelly each day in an attempt to condense his lifetime of horse knowledge into just a few days. Quint thought that the more training Jelly accepted, the greater the chance that Rider would safely return to his home.

As a well respected trainer of horses in the southwestern U.S., Quint never seemed to be able to differentiate between his horse 'children' and his human child. In Quint's mind, a well trained horse was attained when it is dutiful and values his riders' directives above its own instinct, while a well trained daughter is attained when she develops an independent mind based on the 'ground training'.

Quint had expected his daughter would be his best 'horse', but she turned out to be his best child, which Quint viewed as bad training and abandonment. When she broke out of his corral to start a life of her own, he wrote her off in every place but his heart. It was years prior to his tracheotomy but on the day she left he should have reveled in the culmination of his training, rather than creating a similar hole in his heart when he abandoned her due to his fear of being alone and rejected. On that day, unknowingly, he also cut his own throat.

-10-

Pig Island

The first streaks of dawn guided Rider to a small ranch outside of Lordsburg, New Mexico. There was an open pen amongst the other ten horses in the shed, so Jelly had a home out of the heat of the day. After tending to Jelly, Rider stowed his gear at the back of the barn to sleep out the heat of the day also for it had been a long night getting through and past the remnants of Shakespeare. Making a bed in the shade, he was determined to stay awake to greet the hostler who was sure to appear soon. The decision to pass through Lordsburg at night had already been made. There was a highway and a collection of train tracks to cross, and going through rather than around a town was a much easier task. Towns are usually surrounded by wannabe ranchers with city mindsets about wanderers, and their associated miles of barbed wire and electric fences are unfriendlier still. Rider felt more comfortable dealing with closing time stragglers from the town bar's than haughty and clueless suburbanites. Arousing numerous barking dogs and explaining his travels to wannabe's leading dull lives was not how Rider wanted to spend his evening. He wanted to get through the maze quick and easy.

A little after 6am the ranch foreman, Hobbs, came to the barn for his chores. In his late fifties, Hobbs was of a solid wisp of a man who figured he had spent 75% of his life in a saddle and seemed glad of it. He said little, appreciated the help with chores and told Rider of the trail to the Gila River. Hobbs was content as hell with his life and if he ever stepped foot outside of his home country, it was one step he didn't intend to make. This stubbornness enveloped his outlook on life also, and was tolerant of few others. His vision of life had cost him a couple wives, which was just fine with him-Lordsburg had its share of injun whores. His world was just fine with him, the rest be damned. Working

34

the ranch from a saddle, he well knew the risk and work of being astride in a desert and while he wished Rider well, but wanted no part of it. Feed, water, shade and luck were offered as was polite in the backcountry, but beyond sound information, little more.

Hobbs said that Rider would hit the Gila River in about forty miles, two or three days ride at most, and that there was a little used dirt road he could follow. The river being outside of his country, he couldn't be sure. Rider decided to try for the river in one long hard day hoping to earn a day off lounging next to a river he hoped was really there. Rider carried no maps, because he didn't want to. In the old days, wanderers relied on information gleaned from those they met along the trail and by reading the land. Out of the vanity of proving he could also get along without the modern convenience of a map, Rider wanted to do it the same.

At 10pm Rider got itchy, saddled up and walked Jelly toward town. By midnight he had slipped through town unnoticed and walked behind a slow moving freight train until he found a safe place to cross. He had kinda comically hoped he would have passed by a drunk or two just to see their reaction to an apparition to an old buckskin clad Mountain man walking through town in the middle of the night, but Rider didn't run across any that he knew of. Once out of town and heading north the terrain soon became littered with boulders but eventually he found the road Hobbs had mentioned. After another mile the road turned into a path, then a trail, and then nothing. The moonlight was more than sufficient for travel and what started out as a wide peaceful valley was fast becoming a canyon. As the canyon walls crept closer, peaceful and safe was becoming pointed and risky. When the canyon narrowed to a steep draw, the thought of retracing his steps was being reluctantly considered. Night was waning right along with Rider's energy and resolve. The temperature hovered around 40F and the stillness of the night was deafening. Rider loosened the cantel pigging strings to grab his blanket which he quickly fashioned into a poncho for warmth and to ward off cactus protectors. He found himself in a snarl of 10' tall mesquite branches which bit beast and man with each step. Tying an exasperated Jelly, Rider scouted ahead searching for a game trail leading to the river he hoped was really there. In this land of smaller animals, game trail swaths were 5' tall at best, making the going tough for a hunched over Rider.

Travel through sharp edged mesquite was painful for a much taller Jelly, his eyes and nose were being continually skewered. Rider slowly worked his way through the tangles and as night struggled with dawn he spied the river about a quarter mile away. From this place the canyon wall on the left rose vertically to the horizon and on the right a dry stream bed fell away from the wash so abruptly that a unicorn might have to struggle to get a drink. Rider determined that by the time he could lead Jelly this far the horse would be able to sniff the water and work his way to it on his own.

Jelly was sound asleep on three legs when Rider returned to fetch him. On his return he did his best to clear a swath so Jelly could pass through in some degree of comfort. Rider was especially watchful for branches that could lodge underneath the saddle or cinch, which could actually impale the horse. Rider grabbed his extra shirt out of his saddlebags and tied it around Jelly's eyes and ears for protection from the natural arrows. Jelly made it through alright and now Rider was trying to figure out how to actually get to the river as the wash severely narrowed. It looked like Jelly would have to grow wings or die of thirst with the water in sight. Rider considered turning back to where the canyon splayed out a bit and hunting another approach, but weighed that against the worn out condition of himself and his horse. They blew through the last patch of mesquite and Jelly was out of his mind from being stabbed and poked in the 30 minutes it took. Rider was sticky hot and covered in mesquite bark, but like Jelly, thankful to still have both eyes. Moving forward out of the mesquite now within a stone's throw to the river, they discovered a last impediment, a 25' vertical drop to the water.

They had made it to the Gila, at least close enough to look at. The water was crystal clear and appeared as an apparition, but the gurgling sound of water was reassuring. The Gila was a tame twenty foot wide river snaking through a quarter mile wide riverbed. The riverbed provided foreboding evidence as to how violent this quiet stream could be during a flashflood. Jelly was just as desperate to roll around in the cool flowing water as Rider. There was, however, the small matter of getting from point A to point B, with a 25' cliff at their toes. The water both had been drinking for the past two weeks and 150 miles had been primarily from seeps and scum-topped stock tanks, so getting to the river and its clear drinking water was especially enticing.

Jelly still had the spare shirt wrapped around his head but had been skewed enough by the branches so he could now plainly see that which he had been sniffing for the past couple hours. Picking bits of branches and bark out of his scalp, clothes and skin, Rider did the same for his horse while pondering the task of descending the sandy cliff at their feet. Visions of lazing along the river's edge, eating fresh fish and soaking his feet enticed like a siren wailing from the surrounding hills. He was convinced Jelly was fantasizing also. Jelly's feet could use a good soaking too. Just downriver from where they stood was a small island of bright green lush grass smack dab in the middle of the flow. At present, Rider counted eleven javalinas, the southwest's wild pig, contentedly grazing without knowing of Rider's gaze. These amazing creatures possess a furtive character that belies their edgy appearance. Everything about a javelina is tough and sharp, from their porcupine-like hair to their menacing tusks. They can stand dead still without even a detectable breath for hours if need be. The perfect desert machine.

Being upwind and above, Rider watched as the pigs enjoyed grazing on their own little island. Rider decided to delay the soon-to-be arduous task of getting Jelly to water in favor of a little fun. He called out to the pigs, chided them for allowing a lowly human being to sneak up on them, and let out a loud guffaw for good measure. The pigs tucked in their butts and jumped from their dinner plates, squealed and farted their responses directed toward one so rude. All in good fun of course!

Reluctantly returning to the task at hand, Rider still had not found any inspiration of how to persuade his 1200 pound horse to leap off a 25' sand cliff, even though he knew Jelly could do it without injury. Rider decided that he had two choices, pull or push. The 'pulling' choice had the decided negative of the horse landing on top of him, and the 'pushing' choice had the likely negative of getting the crap kicked out of him.

Since Jelly had broken Rider's spine once already by landing on him, Rider chose the latter. Rider figured that he had opposable thumbs for a reason, and that evolutionary advantage ought to trump any hooves directed at his skull. Unbeknownst to Rider, while he was pondering with his perceived intellectual advantages, Jelly had already taken a peek over the cliff and evidently determined that dying of thirst was a better option than growing wings and had backed away from the cliff until the mesquite penetrating his butt hurt too badly. Rider shucked his shirt and rolled it into a blindfold. Upon seeing this, Jelly began searching for escape routes. He might be a horse, but not a dumb horse. Jelly refused Rider's attempt to readjust the blindfold by rearing up, so Rider altered his approach. As he began to remove the saddle, Jelly calmed down a bit. Rider tied the saddle to Jelly's mecate, (halter rope), about a foot away from the horse's nose, and after a while the dangling saddle began to get heavy on Jelly's nose. Meanwhile Rider began kicking off the edge of the cliff decreasing the height but also the angle of the precipice. Still tiring from a saddle hanging off his nose, Jelly's head sank lower and lower toward the ground. Rider began to brush Jelly and worked around the horse cleaning hooves and talking softly to no one in particular. He fetched his canteen, filled his leather hat and placed it in front of Jelly's muzzle, slowly moving the hat toward the edge. He filled the hat again and placed the hat on the ground near the cliff edge, a little too close for Jelly's liking, but he was very thirsty. Rider set again to the brushing and hoof cleaning routine as if there was not a care in the world.

Rider synchronized his movements with the horses brain; kind of like knowing when a child is about to cry even though the kid doesn't know it yet. By the time Jelly had convinced himself to take a couple steps toward the water-filled hat, dragging the dead weight of the saddle from his nose, Rider had innocently moved his brushing to Jelly's back legs.

At the bottom of the cliff lying on his belly with all four legs splayed out, Jelly now looked like a cartoon character. He was too scared to even shiver. Rider would never have been able to con a mule like he just conned Jelly. Mules are bastardly critters that seem to savvy everything. But Jelly was a horse all by himself.

The last thing Jelly remembered, it seemed, was lifting his rear leg just a smidge so he could stretch to the water in the hat. It was in that moment that Rider, his buddy and pal, drove his shoulder into Jelly's haunches and launched the young horse into the atmosphere. Rider snatched up his hat, poured the water over his head to cool off, slid down the hill and untied the saddle from Jelly's nose. All the while trying to convince the horse that he had absolutely no idea how they both got to where they now stood.

Must have been the result of opposable thumbs.

11.

Harry

Nothing fazed Harry Fralie.

No problem in the world existed without a corresponding solution. Some solutions were well hidden, then sought and discovered only by those with the brains and persistence to discover them. Failure to find these solutions was never an option. This was Harry.

Harry was somewhere north of 60 years old and had also worked as a small town cop, or deputy or some such. Any hair that could be seen was salt n' pepper but if there was more on his topknot, it would remain a mystery forever because that's how long Harry kept his sweat stained straw cowboy hat on his noggin'. Above his breastplate and below his belt Harry could still pass for half his age, but the rounded beer supplied growth sheltering his cajones from the weather outed his true vintage. He liked to qualify his beer gut by saying that all good equipment should be stored under cover. Of his ten fingers he still had a little more than nine, losing most of that digit to a rawhide lariat dallied around a pommel while the loop was cinched to a disagreeable bull. He said he never felt it go, and had gotten to a whiskey bottle soon enough to have never needed even to wince.

It was doubtful that Harry could walk unless his feet were lovingly wrapped in cowboy boots. As Quint's best friend, Harry seemed perpetually frustrated by the only challenge in life that he couldn't fix, Quint's relationship with his daughter. In 50 years of friendship, Harry never was able to contrive a solution to convince Quint that people could not be trained like horses. Like stilling a runaway horse, Harry confided that he never mustered the guts to lay his molars into Quint's ear a long time ago, so Quint would shut up long enough to see his love for his daughter through the fog of his own insecurity. In the month that Rider stayed on the

Last Penny, he and Harry chatted often about Quint and his daughter. Quint's sala, or den, was a veritable shrine to all the horse shows his daughter had competed in and dominated throughout the region. The situation reminded Rider of the famous Shakespearean tragedy, Othello. Quint the little pistol of a horse trainer had obstinately turned himself into a jackass as Desdemona wondered why. Harry loved Quint's family and while Quint was ruining it from within, Harry could never bring himself to slap Quint into reality. All that would have accomplished was more withdrawal and hatred from Quint, or so thought Harry. So Harry chose the silent approach with his best friend while staying close with Quint's family and acting as a conduit. He always hoped that by some miracle that Quint would come to his better senses, and repair fences. By the time Quint had mellowed with age, the surgeons removed his cajones to do so, along with his larynx. Nothing would change other than Quint quieting himself for longer periods of time while Harry was talking about Quint's grandkids that Quint rarely saw. Neither Harry nor Quint had much faith or respect for those younger. These old cowboys lived in a world that was, not was to be, and that did not bother either of them one whit. Younger folks were soft, expected reward without work, and quit too easily. To men like Quint and Harry, hard work, toughness and persistence were biblical requisites for adulthood and respect. While Rider was fixing up Last Penny and allowing time for Jelly to get acclimated to the desert, Harry voluntarily modified Rider's buffalo hide moccasins for the desert and modified his saddle and added pigging strings. Knives got expertly sharpened, and his pistol was cleaned and oiled better than it ever had been. In Rider, Harry found a like spirit and celebrated his apparent resolve. Maybe all the young ones weren't wimps after all. Harry had spent more than enough desert days in the saddle and well knew the trials Rider would face as he struck out across the desert.

It had been 24 days since Rider, with his spiffed up outfit thanks to Harry, had tipped his hat to Quint, Harry, and the patched up fences of the Last Penny Ranch.

12.

Redrock

While saddling a still-stunned Jelly, Rider was cajoling his horse into believing that he was in fact, a horse and not a gnarly old mule too obstinate to walk. Mules were like that. Once they decided that 'here' was just fine, there was no prayer of getting to another 'here' until said mule decided such.

Not moving, no way, no how. That is a mule.

Jelly was a horse now convinced he was a mule, or perhaps still too scared to take a step. The last step he took he went airborne down a twenty-five foot cliff. Even as the cool, crystal clear, shallow Gila River bubbled by, Jelly was still trying to wrap his brain around the scrambled recent events. Rider looped the reins around the saddle horn, knowing Jelly would eventually follow, (albeit somewhat reluctantly), and searched the river banks for a nesting spot. He found a nice cut bank just downstream of the newly named Pig Island and made preparations to laze out the remainder of the day. Fashioning a lean-to against the bank thirty feet from shore, Rider was out of sight and sun for the day. A long night warranted a long sleep. Stripped of his gear, Jelly was contentedly munching on the first green grass he had seen since getting in the trailer back in the State of Washington for the trip south. Jelly was still figuring out the hobbles on his front legs, and Rider was wondering if there would be any grass left for the javelina's with some amusement.

Rider was looking forward to the next day's travel as the hills to the north seemed green with grass to feed his horse. He also figured he was about 100 miles north of the border and could relax a bit from the stress of avoiding drug runners.

Along about dusk, Rider evidently felt it was time for a stupid idea. He had spent the day sleeping, bathing and doing laundry. He had constructed a fish weir in the morning and suppered on some fish he convinced himself were trout. Jelly had enjoyed his day also, eating bathing and rolling around. The mesquite mess was a distant memory. Both horse and rider appreciated the day but were still a mite weary.

With that knowledge Rider simply left Jelly hobbled out on the island for the night, rather than staking him to a ground pin. Rider was convinced that walking hobbled into the spooky river was not going to happen. As said, stupid idea.

It took Rider about two hours to find his horse the following morning. Jelly had walked about 4 miles upstream, which meant that prior to really awakening, Rider had walked about eight. Of course Rider used all of his noted tracking skills and common sense when he started his search in the wrong direction. Riding Jelly bareback returning to the campsite proved to have some merit, as Rider sighted a dirt trail heading north away from the river. The day did not seem that it was going to be a scorcher, and along with being emboldened by finding his horse, Rider suspicioned that a wonderful day was about to be had.

Enjoying some of the fish he had smoked during the previous day for breakfast, Rider casually tacked up and returned his campsite to insignificance. The days' course was set, as he mounted and clambered out of the stream bed heading toward the Gila National forest. Keeping the river on his right, the trail melded into a dirt road and he soon began to pass ruins of houses, fences and barns. He was riding through a long, narrow, though painfully dry, beautiful valley. The Gila River streambed was littered with remains of houses that it had swallowed. The Gila River drowned the ghost town of Redrock for the last time in the early 1900's, as the will of the mines matched the played out resolve of the inhabitants who could not bear to rebuild their town for the nth time, especially since the mines were now producing little. Of the 300 year round families that once called Redrock home, only 12 remained in houses as dated as their owners. The town experienced a small rebirth around 1940, but the Gila and the mines again proved fickle, and the town drowned again. Redrock was a working man's town, it was said, of miners and ranchers. The town somehow escaped harboring the vices and turmoil of the day. Lordsburg was close enough for whoring, drinking and gambling, and, Redrock purposely did not have a bank. The townsfolk decided that their peaceful valley didn't need bank robbers.

13.

Pieces for Peace

A saddle has many uses, an anchor even, but rarely a pillow. That's a Hollywood derivation. After long hours of riding the seat leather is usually moist and smelly, in need of airing out. Even the slightest wind in the desert carries a fog of sand ready to be unleashed on exposed flesh. A saddle set upright with a stake through the gullet makes for a stout, dependable wind break. The fleece underside is also exposed to the air so the wicked moisture of the day's use can dry, preventing rot and mold in the underside leather. Horses do not like the smell of mold any more than they like the smell of blood and maggots. A saddle can make a hell of a backrest, but when the wind picks up in the middle of the night, a savvy caballero rests while others with saddle pillows cuss and struggle to rearrange their nest.

Rider carried a well beaten lever handled Winchester .32 and fifty rounds. He wasn't expecting or hoping for any wars, but fifty was enough to dissuade should the need arise. The .32 was an older bullet and might not have been attainable on his journey, so he felt fifty was a good number. The .32 rifle was a well made, tough gun. It had a walnut stock and enough power to down a small deer at thirty yards. The firing and chambering mechanisms were simple, easily cleaned, and rarely jammed. Keeping a sandbox out of the mechanism was about all that was required for the rifle to function. Lastly, the gun doubled as a garden tool, or hammer in a pinch, though Mr. Winchester might be disgusted with such treatment. The exterior was scratched, pitched and gouged, but the mechanism and barrel was always well oiled.

Tough gun.

Rider carried the Winchester sleeping in its dark leather scabbard underneath his right leg parallel to the earth with the stock forward. He could both feel and see the gun while riding. Had he oriented the weapon in reverse, the gun could be snatched by a branch and he would never know it was lost until he reached down for it, only to learn it had spilled out 'somewhere' back along the trail. He was not willing to take the risk. The scabbard was rigged fore and aft, (front and back for you landlubbers), on D-rings attached to the saddle skirt underneath the seat so the gun wouldn't slap Jelly in the ribs with each step. The gun was oriented upside down with the trigger facing him, as well as the crook where the stock met the steel, so the angle assisted the effort to withdraw the weapon from the saddle. With the weapon facing aft and downward the risk of shooting his horse in the ass, or himself in the foot, were minimal, but hey, shit happens.

Rider always had a round chambered, as well as four rounds reserved in the stock. He had modified the hammer by heating it and then bending it over at a seventy degree angle to give his thumb better purchase, and so as not to interfere with sighting. A quick thumbing of the hammer, a gentle squeeze of the trigger was all that was required. Rider felt that should he survive the journey and make it home, he'd likely find forty rounds remaining in his kit. Any less would mean that he had lived through some kind of trouble. His spare rounds he kept dry and clean, and split the load by placing some in each saddlebag and a few on his belt so he would never be left without ammo.

He never took a single step without his pistol or rifle on his person. One could never anticipate the spooked horse, the broken leg, or any number of other events that might occur that would leave one in a severe survival situation. On his right hip he carried a .22 Magnum revolver, riding high on his hip-he wasn't planning any duels. It was chambered with two snake shot rounds, followed by three slugs. The hammer rode on an open chamber, so if it fell and hit a rock, it wouldn't discharge by mistake. The Rider had not only heard of this practice, he had seen it with this gun. Pistols have a tendency to jump out or be yanked out of their holsters by a branch at the most inopportune moments. This weapon was also simplistic in its design, and not very susceptible to malfunctions even when dirty. The chamber was removable, and the firing mechanism well exposed. It was a single action weapon, meaning the hammer had to be thumbed back to fire each round. He had performed the same alteration on this hammer as he had on the rifle.

Rider had considered a rifle and pistol that fired the same rounds, but soon gave up the idea due to the extra weight of a larger pistol. In the olden days, a rifle and a pistol had similar purposes, killing men if need be. Rider doubted that the first thing to come to mind of any person that sighted him was going to robbery, therefore the need for a man-killing pistol was not likely. The pistol was for snakes, rodents and for sufficiently discouraging those with ill intent. As with the Winchester rounds the small .22 cartridges were dispersed between each saddlebag and his belt. The rifle was for securing a large amount of food with one bullet, just in case he found himself in that situation, or for discouraging predators, 2-4 legged alike.

His weapons were only effective against bad guys at close range, and Rider was determined to keep his distance.

14.

To Gamble

By scanning the terrain to the north, Rider could tell he had a decision to make. That decision, would likely dictate the kind of life he would be living for the next few days. To the north, in the direction he wanted to go, were a hob glob of gentle mountain peaks, forested by dull, green trees. Dull meant thirsty, meaning that was exactly what horse and rider would be, should that choice be made. The mishmash of peaks meant for hard riding, as no clear channel through the hills was evident. The mountain choice meant lots of extra miles continually criss-crossing canyons and skirting peaks. The river headed off in a northeasterly direction, for what the Rider could see was a greater distance by a long shot, and he wasn't sure that he wanted to deviate from his destination direction. However the river made for seemingly easier, safer and more tolerable travel. That choice however contained a great risk. The gamble was that if he found himself in a canyon or gorge, he might not be able to get out of it, or he could be swept away by a flash flood birthed in some distant mountains. It seemed the safest choice was to head into the mountains, ride a hard day in the heat, and travel again by night, even though mountain travel at night is much slower than in the flat desert. Weighing the options, mountain travel was the smart choice, but Rider didn't opt for that. Jelly high stepped like he was in a parade, as he splashed his way straight up the middle of the river. The sun was bright, the water cool, and the scenery magnificent.

The sirens had called, and Rider had answered. This day would make the vicissitudes at the mesquite draw seem paltry. Had he only known, alas, his guts had told him, he just didn't listen, and the stress and sufferings they were heading into were not to be pleasant. Not only was the river getting narrow and faster flowing, but they were also climbing. Rider could never see too far ahead as the river wound out of the hills.

They had been river walking for two hours, and Rider was fascinated by the sharp cliffs and the turquoise water. What earlier had been small stepping stones were now developing into obstacles for the horse. They splashed their way around a bend to find a waterfall that Rider was sure Jelly could negotiate going upstream, but was just as positive he would break a leg trying it the other way. Rider tied Jelly to a branch on shore, took off his shirt and waded upstream hoping to find a swale or draw they could utilize to climb out of the canyon. He had been scanning the hillsides on the north side of the river for some time. He waded upstream until it was obvious the canyon was only getting narrower, indicating that a scramble up a cliff or retracing their steps were the two choices. Scrambling up a vertical cliff was going to be hot, time consuming and dangerous. First, he couldn't see the canyon rim, and he had been fooled by canyon rims in the past. Typically one rim was scaled only to reveal another just as high, and so on. Second, they might find themselves on a ledge that a horse could not negotiate, leaving Jelly to figure out a way back down to the river, or stand there and die. That the horse would make it to the river on his own, given time, Rider had no doubt. 'Given time', was the operative phrase. The day, already having been dictated by poor decisions, was growing hotter.

Rider eyed a swale in the cliffside on the other side of the river from where they now stood. A swirling deep pool ricocheting off a huge boulder stood in the way. He shed his clothes and waded upstream far enough so that when he ventured out into the river, he might be across before the current slammed him into the

48

boulder. A fairly easy and somewhat refreshing short swim later, he started to scale and scout the cliff to see if Jelly could negotiate it. He kept climbing until he convinced himself that although there were some risky, steep sections, he really didn't have a choice. Jelly would have to climb. Scrambling back down the hillside, Rider reversed the swimming process to rejoin Jelly. He was going to have to ride Jelly as far up the river as possible prior to entering the current. He pondered as he packed his gear, and realized that if his horse lost balance or froze, they both would surely be smashed against the boulder.

He considered another option. He could spur Jelly to jump directly into the pool and by the time Jelly had made his first swim stroke, they might be able to use the current and boulder to their advantage by leaning against it, and wedging themselves past the current. In this method, the risk was they would not reach enough of the boulder by the time Jelly surfaced from the first jump. This was the method chosen, and without another ponder, Rider swung himself astride, yelled, 'Cha hah', kicked and slapped Jelly who in turn leaped out into the swirling pool. Jelly's head went clear under the water so far that Rider, still astride, could barely see his ears. As the horse broke the surface with a thrust that smacked the Rider's loins, the current took hold of the now partially surfaced horse, and shoved them against the boulder just as the Rider's left foot cleared the leather tapadera covering the stirrup, avoiding injury. Jelly rested for a split second, and with another, 'Cha hah', the horse took another great thrust, found purchase, and climbed out on the other side of the river.

Knowing that spending the night in a narrow, boxed canyon was not an option in flash flood country, Rider inspected all his gear, retied, and plotted the task of scaling the cliff. He tied the hobble rope to Jelly's bosal and coiled the length in his hand, preparing to play it out when Jelly needed more space to climb. The long scramble upward began. Every 50' or so, horse and man would find a semblance of a flat spot, rest and inspect the next move. At one point Rider, leading the horse had to quickly sit on the rope to assist the horse from falling backward head over heels. He was hoping they were making a suitable commotion to discourage any self-respecting rattlesnake from investigating the activity. After three hours of scrambling up and through sharp, loose rocks, cactus and other nasties, they topped the last ridge with about an hour of daylight left.

Finding a small sandstone bench surrounded by tar brush, Rider tethered Jelly, unsaddled and quickly spread out his gear to dry. It was going to be a moist sleep, but he hoped the waning sunlight would dry out his gear more than less. He started a fire and set some jerky on a nearby rock to warm and soften.

There were a few patches of dull green grass within eyeshot so he gathered a half dozen of these and laid them in front of Jelly to munch on while he rubbed the horse down. Jelly was played out and a bit dehydrated, as Rider could tell by taking a pinch of his skin to see how fast it returned. If the skin doesn't snap back immediately, the horse needs water. Speaking of water, Rider's canteen had leaked during the pull up the cliff, and only about two cups of water remained.   By looking at the mountains to the north and reading the configuration, he figured the next canyon with water was about thirty miles away. That's a lot of miles for two cups of water, he thought.

Darkness comes slow to the high desert, about 4000' where he was, so he had ample time to treat all the cuts and scratches for both horse and himself that the cliff ascent had produced. Given the water situation, Rider had already decided that they would move off as soon as the moon provided enough light to see. A few hours of rest was in order until that time, and both did.

Rider figured he had slept about four hours and judged it to be about 2am when he saddled Jelly. Both staggered through the soreness of the previous day. In about thirty minutes they were sufficiently warmed and the night shaped up to be rather pleasant, albeit chilly. Rider preferred to walk in front of his horse on this night, knowing the difficulty of the previous day. Keeping the river on his right, to the east, and the North Star smiling brightly, likely chilled also, Rider felt he could keep to the ridge and shave needless miles off this part of the journey. The ridge seemed to travel in the same direction Rider was heading so he was quite content to follow along. He also knew that if thirst became a great danger, he could always head back down to the river, and worry about getting back out later.

It was an easy stroll and Rider enjoyed the conversation with his horse amidst the clip-clop of hooves. Home improvement projects back on the ranch, their Boxer dogs they missed, pizza and women were the typical conversation subjects, though not necessarily in that order. One particular chat about a ballerina who liked to point her toes with her legs in a perfect perpendicular position from her hips while rutting with a certain gent of immediate recollection, was abruptly interrupted by Jelly letting out an involuntary snort and immediate halt.

Horse ears pricked forward, head tilted and eyes wide, the comforting hand of Rider quickly found the horse's nose, always remembering their secret bond forged from weathering many storms and nasties back on the ranch. Both stood stock still and waited for whatever spook that lay ahead to expose itself. Once adjusted to the light, Rider could confirm the smell the new breeze just brought, and he could make out the shapes of dozens of bedded cattle. These high country cattle were contently sleeping in a tight bunch for warmth and safety. No cougar it its right mind would attempt a kill in such conditions for the bulls would kick the shit out of it. The cattle simply paid no mind to the smell of a horse. Of all the luck, bunched cattle usually meant water, and sure enough they had come upon a spring! Jelly snuck in three good gulps before Rider was able to shush the horse away so he could drink his fill without ingesting horse snot. Looping the reins and mecate around the saddle horn, Rider then let Jelly loose to drink his fill. As the first streaks of the new day brushed the sky, Rider mounted and they left the spring, replenished and relieved.

At mid-morning the ridge trail had turned south for too long for Rider to tolerate, so they cut trail in a northerly direction. Taking a side trip to the top of a rise so he could scan the countryside, Rider was able to pick out Redrock far to the south but nothing else of note so he turned Jelly in a northerly direction to see what the day would bring. After a leisurely mile Rider caught a glimpse of the river still flowing in the direction it was supposed to, and an obviously lived-in shack. With the heat of the day coming on, and the river looking way too inviting he chose to head that way. A valley led to the river and even though it was a couple miles east, the occupant(s) of the shack might be kind enough to provide information about the country heading north. It was near noon when Rider hailed the shack.

'Hank', obviously coming off yet another good drunk stumbled out of the shack, none too pleased to be awakened so early in the day. Being careful not to pee on the left leg of his gray oft peed on stained pants while leaning against the door jamb, the 58 year old got friendlier with each awakening brain cell. Shirtless, bath deprived and beer bellied, Hank gave his pecker a couple tugs and tucked it back in his pants, zipped only high enough to keep it from popping out. Rider thought that it might have been years since Hank had actually seen his pecker, given his obvious daily routine. A cowboy by trade, but too busted up, old and drunk to keep him on cowboy wages, the McCauley Ranch kept him on the payroll to watch over the southern access to the substantial ranch. Sipping on lukewarm coffee while watching Jelly graze nearby, Hank said that he hadn't seen a human for a month. Rider was thankful that Jelly had some feed, declined the offer of coffee stirred with a urine soaked finger, and rested in the shade while Hank told stories between dozes. He talked of the McCauley's mostly, and the family's relationships with the Earp's, John Slaughter, Kit Carson and other notable Old

West characters.

Just before dusk Hank scratched out a map in the dirt that depicted the trails toward the northern border of the ranch near Cliff, New Mexico. He said that he hadn't been up to the north edge in more than a decade, but allowed that if any of the springs he had told Rider about had dried up he would have heard about it. As the first batch of stars finally appeared Rider gathered his sun-dried gear, bade thanks and goodbye to a passed out Hank, and walked Jelly about a mile north before making a dry camp along the river's edge. He drank a lot of water because he wanted biology or his pee alarm as he called it, to wake him up for an early start.

By the time the sun rose in earnest Rider had been three hours into the pine trees enjoying a cool, sunny day. Hank's dirt map, complete with landmarks was in Rider's mind as he picked his way north through terrain he later learned was a haven for lost smokejumpers. The maze of trails worn by generations of cattle made navigating the country unusually difficult to figure. Seldom was there flat land that stretched for more than a quarter mile. The coolness of the day allowed them to press on and Jelly was as eager as Rider. Rider walked one mile for every four ridden. During these strolls the saddle was always loosened a bit and shifted to allow air to get to Jelly's back; a sore backed horse takes a long time to heal. Rider enjoyed walking but if he wrecked his horse he did not wish to have to walk all the way home to Washington!

Late in the afternoon he spied a cross road next to a vacant county fairground in the distance and headed for it. Jelly found himself in a nice big pen with Rider bedded in the corner. To Rider, one of life's great treasures was when Jelly would nuzzle him in the middle of the night; sleeping in a corral allowed for that to happen. He paid a curious boy to fetch a couple flakes of alfalfa and some fresh water. Across the dirt road Rider strolled into an empty tavern hoping for a meal. To his delight he found that he had entered the back door and there was an asphalt road in front, meaning that he was indeed *someplace*.

To his further delight the tavern owner appeared, allowed that she was open and that he was standing in Cliff, New Mexico. He and Jelly must have not realized how much ground they had actually covered, but there was no complaining! After a sumptuous meal of steak and potatoes, Rider finished his third beer back in the pen with Jelly and bedded down for the night. A banner day it had been, and he figured they deserved a day off.

The next morning was the beginning of a wonderfully lazy day of recovery. A good brushing for Jelly, a freshly filled water bucket and a couple flakes of hay took care of that chore, and Rider then strolled over to the tavern for a 6am breakfast that had to wait for the 7am opening. Rider spent the hour sitting on the front porch cleaning his guns and admiring the traffic-all three of them.

15.

Lita Rose

At 6' tall, flowing salt and pepper hair and piercing blue eyes, Lita Rose was more western than the west itself. Her oversized brass belt buckle had been flipped open by more men than she cared to, or was able, to count or remember, but that didn't bother her none at all. Well kept for 56, even with a Buckhorn beer paunch, she knew she had rough miles on her carcass, but somehow Rider knew she chose each step of the way without caution, and loved every minute of it. Even the multiple rapes and drunken gangbangs had some redeeming qualities. This particular stop in her life found her raising mules and mending saddles. Saddle making and mule training were her Christian trades and she did them as well as they could be done.

A nasty separation from her last man left her perpetually short of funds, but not short of resolve. She just could not get out of her own way this time.

Lita had an opinion…., about everything, and Rider enjoyed the continual banter until it became too tiresome. Mostly Rider agreed with her because she was right and not afraid to say so. Lita had an old Australian Cow saddle collecting dust on the wall of her small leather shop that was fashioned after the US Cavalry McClellan design, and featured a high narrow gullet allowing for more space above Jelly's withers, and she offered to modify it in exchange for some man chores her shop needed. It was about a quarter of the weight of the ranch saddle made by Bob Hickman back home. The Hickman saddle was a piece of artwork, fit Jelly beautifully, but Jelly was losing lots of weight mostly because of stress.

Lita was convinced that the light cavalry saddle would be more comfortable for Jelly in the coming months of travel, though a great deal less comfortable for Riders' butt. It just meant that Rider was going to walk a greater portion of the 2000 mile trek home rather than ride. Lita was right, as usual. While Lita modified the Aussie saddle to fit Jelly, Rider set to chores around her shop for the next week. It was a good trade and Lita and Rider became plutonic pals. On the morning Rider decided to get back on the trail, Lita and her daughter mounted their mules and guided him through the Sacatone drainage of the Gila Wilderness. Both had worked for cougar hunting guides as cooks and wranglers for years in that part of the country and knew it well. They saved Rider a lot of confusion and anguish getting through that snarl until the flat desert reappeared. They made camp near a sizeable spring and enjoyed a chilly night. At some point during the night Jelly slipped out of his high line halter and wandered off from the mules. Rider called his name and within a minute he came trotting over the rise with his head cocked to one side and all full of himself. He had been playing in the mud and the spring and was raring to go. "Goodbye's" and "Thank you's" were exchanged and, after a good animal brushing session, Lita and her daughter headed south while Rider headed north, again having no idea what was over the next hill or around the next bend.

The day was cool and sunny; a perfect day. At mid-afternoon Rider crested a little rise overlooking a long narrow valley. Near the base of the valley was a collection of buildings that could have been a small town, so Rider took the chance that it might be and headed for it. As soon as they dropped off the rise he lost sight of the buildings but headed in that direction. After an hour of picking his way through the desert pine trees and prickly pear cactus, Rider found himself sitting in a small café in the little town of Glenwood, New Mexico.

Glenwood began as a ranch in the late 1800's and then it became a stage stop, and finally became a town. The handful of locals inside repeated the same warnings about riding into the Indian Nations alone that he had listened to since he first mounted up a month previous. Rider was continually warned that his horse would get stolen, he would be shot on site because of the color of his skin, or that small bands of drunken Indians would harass him and his carcass would never be found. Rider took it all in politely, but he was heading home, and home was north. If the Nations were between him and home, so be it.

Finishing an early supper he untied Jelly from a nearby post and led him up the canyon to find a place to sleep. This particular canyon was of note because back when the mines above were functioning, the miners constructed a 'catwalk' attached to the side of the north canyon wall. This elevated boardwalk snaked its way up a very narrow portion of the canyon to get to the mines and also allowed miners to maintain a wooden water pipe they had constructed to serve an ore crushing mill near the base of the canyon. It was quite an engineering feat for the late 1800's and tools of the day.

Rider poked around for a couple hours because he had a couple hours until the sun would get switched off, and he liked to try to figure out the how's and why's of such unique endeavors. With Jelly hobbled and chowing on a small grassy island in the middle of the canyon creek, Rider scaled the cliff to reach the catwalk to take a closer peek. He allowed that whatever had been mined must have been plenty valuable. Moreover, the vision, effort and resolve required to construct such an apparatus in such a remote and inaccessible place verified their spirit. Having satisfied his curiosity and knowing that nights come quickly in the high desert, he scrambled back down the cliff, fetched up Jelly and moved a few hundred yards up the creek to make a cold, but comfortable camp.

16.

First Visitor

The evening was as peaceful as an evening could be.

Rider was able to procure a pint of whiskey, a couple cigars, a used paperback book and a bottle of Coke; which he stuck in the creek to keep chilled. A clear starry night in cool mountain air, good feed and water for Jelly, and the reflection of the moon off the cliffside was bright enough for Rider to read his book without the aid of a campfire or a small flashlight. A plastic cup of chilled whiskey and coke, and a smooth cigar made for a perfect evening. Thoughts of home back on Rattlesnake Breaks Ranch in Washington came mighty easy on this night.

A rustle of leaves caught Rider's attention along about midnight. Opening his eyes and ears while laying still, he could sense eyes upon him. He could hear Jelly quietly munching a short distance away. There it was again, only now Rider heard a slight scuff down near his feet. Slowly lifting his head he spied two sparkling eyes reflected from the moonlight staring right at him only 10' away. As he slowly lifted his revolver the animal scampered away into the woods, turned around and stared at him again. The eyes and behavior was not right for a cougar-even a young one-though these mountains were full of them he had been told. It moved too fast for a raccoon but the eyes were similar. The animal circled every so often and soon Rider caught glimpses in the moonlight. Jelly had stopped munching and was standing stock still. The critter was about 3' long from nose to the end of the tail and no more than a foot tall at the shoulder. Rider had never seen such a critter, and didn't know if it was aggressive or not. It kept its distance but hung around so Rider figured that he would do what his horse did, and that was to go back to doing what they were doing; Jelly munching and Rider sleeping. A short while later the critter woke Rider up again by sniffing his feet. As soon as Rider lifted his head, the critter would again scamper off.

This little game persisted for about an hour until Rider chucked a few rocks at it in the hopes that the critter would be dissuaded from returning. He didn't want to shoot his new pal but Rider needed sleep and the critter wanted to continue to investigate.

Somewhere in New Mexico there is a critter with half a tail. Rider shot the other half off, and slept soundly the rest of the night. A few days later Rider learned that the mysterious critter was a Ringtail, or Miner's Cat, even though it is not a cat at all. Back in the mining days, it is told that some miners would capture and domesticate ringtails, and that some of the animals went into the mines with their pals as 'air testers', much like was done with canaries in coal mines that would die in their cages so the miners knew to get out of the mines before meeting the same fate. Some say that so many Ringtails were domesticated that curiosity and seeming lack of fear is generational learned behavior.

Rider later pondered that maybe the critter just wanted to snuggle and all he got was his ass shot off for his attempted affectionate advances. Rider mused that most men could relate.

17.

Eating Ground

It was a cool, crisp morning and they had covered 12 miles of ground by noon. Both Rider and Jelly were feeling vigorous and strong on this day as they slowly emerged from the hill country. Rider began to get glimpses of the flat high desert country to the north through the branches. The folks back in the Glenwood Café said that he had about a good two day ride to reach the town of Luna, New Mexico. Beyond Luna he would have about a hundred mile pull of flat sand until he could expect to find water, given the drought conditions. Rider always appreciated such offers of knowledge when he received it, but knew that the information was never from the actual perspective astride a saddle, but rather from either behind a steering wheel or outright hearsay. A body notices things differently from a saddle versus through a windshield. A simple thirty minute drive might take a horseman all day to match, depending on the terrain. In any event, Rider knew the upcoming terrain was too flat to show any guiding landmarks and would likely be without water. There was a dangerous stretch to come and the ease of travel of the last few days was going to be a very distant memory. If he had enough of a moon they could get started at dusk and set Jelly to a comfortable ground eating trot.

Late afternoon the next day they strolled into the small old sheep village of Luna, New Mexico. Rider dismounted and tied Jelly under a shade tree and dropped the saddle and upturned blankets nearby to dry. The past sixteen hours had been dry but tolerable; lots of dust accumulated on Rider, Jelly and the gear. As with many small western settlements, the only café in town served as post office, store, booze shop, and the like. After finishing a meal that 'could be beat', Rider walked Jelly about one mile north of town and found a tolerable place to camp near a stock tank with running water and enough grass nearby that Rider could collect in a pile for Jelly.

The next morning he quickly found an old mail route trail that had been described to him by a gent in the café. It turned out to be a cool day and to Rider's great comfort and relief, they dropped into a swale that accommodated the old trail for a good portion of the day. The swale sometimes had shade and sometimes had water. Toward the first hint of dusk, Rider spied an old barn and a shack with a stock tank that was obviously full. The barn held some mostly molded alfalfa hay bales from a season past, and after skimming off a couple inches of scum layer out of the stack tank, he found the water to be quite fresh; the tank had an integral float valve and filled from the bottom somehow. Adding to this unexpected extravagance, the shack had a single mattress hanging from the rafters. Rider would sleep on a mattress for the first time in more than a month! They had covered 30 miles that day and unexpectedly ended up with water, shade, grub and shelter for both. The remaining purported 70 miles to the next inhabited settlement would be reachable likely without much danger since they replenished themselves at this place. As Rider supped on some jerky and nuts while reading, he was considering resting for a day prior to taking on the next 70 miles to the next purported guaranteed water; that being in Fence Lake, New Mexico. He didn't know what he would find in Fence Lake, and no one back in Luna or Glenwood did either. Small outposts like theirs and Fence Lake can quickly fade into ghost town status, and unless some reason for an influx of people is discovered, all their towns were inevitably heading in that direction also.

The water in the stock tank was frozen solid the next morning when Rider emerged from the toasty little line shack. With the drought, cattle prices were so low that many cattlemen simply abandoned what remained of their herds, and Rider suspected that the shack that served this part of the range hadn't been visited for more than a year-likely longer. Jelly cocked his head toward Rider, snorted, and eyed him with the derisive look of a jilted woman because Rider had slept on a cozy mattress while Jelly froze his ass off overnight. Rider kiddingly chastised the horse and slapped his rump a few times just to get the circulation going.

Man and horse wanted to get moving so Rider saddled quickly, neatened up the area and shack and scrawled a note of thanks. The day wasn't shaping up to be a 'chamber of commerce' day as an overcast sky persisted while a cold wind kept up its' hackles. In the early afternoon they came upon a small battered wooden sign pointing to a spring. While winding down the steep old trail Rider held the reins in his left hand while reaching back and grasping the cantel, or the back of the saddle, so his weight would not force his weight and the saddle toward Jelly's neck.   Appaloosa's are well known for their surefootedness, but Jelly's abrupt slip and tumble surprised both of them. Rider cleared the saddle just in time to avoid being an airbag for Jelly's full weight. Both were okay when all settled, but gear repair was in order. Rider's only tool was a 'Super Leatherman' pocket tool clipped to his suspenders over his self made deer hide serape, and the tool served him well. His canteen housing was split but still held water. He'd fix this later by tearing a piece of leather off his serape/poncho, soaking it and drying it in the sun as soon as the sun came back around. The stock of his .32' Winchester rifle had split off from the frame rendering it a pistol grip rifle in effect. He'd repair this in the same manner as the canteen on a later date. He stuck the stock in one of the saddlebags and checked/tightened his gear before proceeding down to the supposed spring.

The spring turned out to be a 1" pipe emptying out into a small adobe tank. It had obviously been in service for years. Off in the distance to the north there seemed to be another old barn, so after drinking their fill Rider led Jelly to it. Lo and behold there were more bales of alfalfa in the barn, and these were nowhere near as moldy as the last batch. Jelly was obviously ecstatic!

Hobbling Jelly and bracing the broken down door open, Rider removed the gear, brushed Jelly down, and sequestered himself on top of the bales. Stepping back outside in the chilly breeze, Rider could see a dark rain squall heading right for them so he chose to make a nest amongst the hay bales and sleep out the night. He knew Jelly wasn't going to stray far from the hay, unless hopping himself back to the spring for a drink. The squall would likely keep the horse inside the small barn anyway. The roof held out the rain and the nest Rider had made was quite toasty all night.

A great basin stood to the north and it would take them all day to cross it. After heading back to the spring in the morning for a fill-up, they headed out on hard-packed ground knowing they could be seen from miles away. Usually Rider held to cover whenever possible, but since there was none for miles, there was no choice in the matter. It was an uneventful day astride a fresh horse and both of them were in good spirits. Reaching the northern edge of the basin he could see a complex of large corrals that were obviously used to separate herds back when cattle prices allowed for such. These corrals had been dormant for months. There were a couple of sheds but the windmill-fed stock tank was dry. A small amount of grass poked through the soil around the tank so Rider grabbed what he could, staked Jelly by driving a curled pin into the ground attached to his right rear leg, and bedded himself down in one of the small sheds. Pouring some canteen water into his leather hat, Jelly sucked three hatfuls. Rider had found a small plastic jug in Luna so he had extra water for himself, as well as another snort for Jelly before heading out in the morning. He figured they would make the next village by tomorrow noon if the folks back in Luna were right.

What he feared might be a difficult stretch of desert to cross a few days ago turned out to be a pleasant experience, what with the constant breeze, adequate feed and water.

He could only imagine trying that ride under three days of hot sun and dried up springs…

18.

New Pals

Just after dawn two lorries pulled into the corrals loaded with cattle. Rider was in the process of stowing his gear when one of the drivers wandered over for a chat. The driver was more cowboy than driver, short and rubber-band lean with a face that hadn't seen a razor for a spell.

Rider spoke first, "Just passing through".

"To where? Name's Ned", introducing himself.

"Washington State. Rider, pleased to meet you", Rider replied extending his hand for a firm handshake.

"Likewise. How long you been asaddle?", Ned replied.

"I mounted up down at the border March 15. Any idea what day it is today?"

"April 20. You been travelin' a little more than a month sounds like. Do you have any idea where you are or what you just rode through?"

Gathering his thoughts for a moment, Rider replied that he thought he had a ½ day ride north to the next settlement, but would appreciate any information Ned might offer.

"Well, Rider, Fence Lake is the nearest store to the north, but it's a good 20 miles from here. Ground is flat though. What you just rode through is Apache lands, and we're standing smack dab in the middle of it right now. I'm not sure that a lone white guy on a horse is the smartest thing to be in these parts".

Rider allowed that Ned and his pals knew their 'whatfor's' a whole lot better than he did and finally replied, 'I savvy cow, you fella's need a hand in trade for some feed for my horse?"

By late morning the trucks had been unloaded and the Momma's and calves separated and bedded down for the midday heat. Rider, Ned and the rest of the cowboy crew hunkered down under one of the sheds and all offered to share any extra in their pokes after learning of Rider's journey. Rider appreciated the offers but declined, preferring information. The wranglers told Rider to be conscious of the date when nearing the reservation border towns, and to stay out of site if possible between the 3rd and 5th of each month, as that is when the Indians receive their Government checks. Rider was puzzled upon hearing this and the cowboys smiled amongst themselves until Ned explained the dynamic to Rider.

"Best as I understand things," Ned began, "lots of Indians or Native Americans if you prefer, receive monthly checks from the US Government in payment for leased lands, mineral rights or from past treaties. They get their checks the first week of each month and go to town to get their cash, pay off their pawn checks and buy booze. The crime rates around the border towns spike up each month about that time, so you might find it best to hunker down and not become a statistic, see?"

Rider thought to himself that this was likely the best information he could have possibly received so far on his journey.

The heat began to relent earlier than expected so Rider saddled up, shook hands all around and rode out. Most of the wranglers wished aloud how they could trade places with Rider, but knew it wasn't ever going to happen for them. As he rode on, he quietly pondered that any information he received would get more accurate the closer he got to whatever clime he was approaching, and he would be cognizant of this for the rest of his journey. Now unknowingly in the middle of the first Indian Reservation of many he was slated to traverse, he remembered the stern warnings about riding in the 'nations' from those 100 miles on his back trail compared to the much more accurate information he just received here in one. He'd store this new knowledge for future climes.

A late lunch was taken on the shore of Salt Lake an hour after leaving his new pals at the corrals. Remnants of a salt producing factory remained as well as some other weathered and baked buildings; a little ghost town in and of itself. The mostly dried up lake was purported to be of spiritual significance to the Zuni Indians, those of the reservation he would soon be entering. Noting the distinct lack of animal tracks heading to the 300 yard wide lake, Rider kept Jelly well away from the water in case it contained poisons. Those of the backcountry always check to see if there is animal sign around a standing body of water prior to partaking; no sign-no drink. The final leg to Fence Lake was not going to be pleasant, or so the cowboys had said. Additionally, the ground between Fence Lake and Gallup, New Mexico 80 miles beyond was not going to be a picnic either. Gallup was the first 'border town' Rider would come to, and the odds were he was going to hit it right around 'allotment check' time. His current plan was to get there before "payday", put up Jelly for a few days and get himself a hotel room for a couple days and a hot shower.

The ride to Fence Lake was a dry one, but in the desert most were. It was so hot on this day that even the cactus seemed to shy away from the sun. Just before mid-day and in the middle of absolutely nothing, Rider came upon a ranch house. A father and teenage son were the only inhabitants. Rider waved and kept going; his instinct overriding neighborliness. This was his human allotment for the day, and that was just fine by him. He had already conversed more in the last 24 hours than he had in the past week and he wanted to give his chitchat button a rest.

In the current land, Rider could see his uptrail for miles through the undulating heat waves. Some folks don't think that heat waves can be seen by the human eye, but then most folks don't sit a horse in the middle of the desert either. Both he and Jelly seemed to be on auto-pilot; just moving forward. Rider enjoyed cutting country, seeing things generally unseen by anyone else. Crossing vast uninhabited country sometimes contained hidden arroyos or gateless barbed wire fences. When facing one of these fences, Rider would ride along the fence in each direction for a few minutes and if no gate was in sight, Rider would create one. He would never cut the wire, but he would pull the staples from enough of the wood posts so he could lay the wire flat on the ground.

Once on the ground he covered the 4-5 strands of barbed wired with his blanket so Jelly could be led over without catching a hoof. Once across he would put the fence up usually in much better condition than he found it. Cutting cross country also avoided the natural chasms that repeated trail usage creates, as well as allowing Rider to explore the mostly unexplored.

This brown endless flatness was dotted with sparse pockets of vegetation that concealed arroyos too deep to cross, and almost could not be seen until upon them. Some of these arroyos extend for miles and some are no more than 10' across but perhaps 20' deep. In a twisted, weird thought it seemed to Rider that the desert put out so much effort to carve and blister the land that when it merges into wetlands or woodlands, as the desert does very quickly, that it simply runs out of gas as if there is nothing left in its tank of nastiness. The desert seems to simply die a quick death, and that was somehow apropos to his thinking.

This concept also reminded Rider of Jelly's famous Arabian granddad, named Fadjur. In horse showing circles, which Rider never thought much of, Fadjur was a champion of champions and lived until almost thirty years old. It was said that the horse was in competition almost til he died and when he failed, he failed quickly-just like the desert. Imagine an arm wrestler forced to within an inch of being pinned, knowing there is no longer any hope of winning yet still struggling and finally succumbing to the sheer force of eventuality in an instant.

The desert lives just like someone caught in it.

19.

Lizard Eyes

The gulf between life and death in the desert is mighty wide, until it isn't. Some say the difference between right and wrong is a fine line. Rider was the kind that considered that 'fine line' to be just as wide as the gulf between life and death in the desert. One either lived or died, or was either right or wrong. That was the code he lived by, without regard for societal consequences or someone's potential hurt feelings. He was a gent of few words and decidedly direct in conversation, not unfriendly, but direct nonetheless.

The people he met in the deserts seemed to appreciate this characteristic about him even though many expected, or were used to compassion or charity about their challenging desert living conditions. Rider offered none. Rider could see the death in their wide eyes upon seeing this seemingly ghostly apparition of a single horse and rider. Not only could Rider detect the death but also the waning hope in their souls. Drought is a cruel method of losing life as well as hope-not necessarily in that order. This drought was killing everything in this country, vultures and coyotes being the exceptions. Farmers were terrified to plant fearing the burden of unharvestable stunted growth of their crop and in their souls. Ranchers were terrified to release their cattle out to the range fearing a chunk of their guts evaporating with every ear tag pulled from an expired thirsted carcass. This was the land Rider was now discovering, as the back trail hadn't been productive for decades for either farmer or rancher; this land was experiencing severe drought for the first time in memory.

Thrusting Jelly to jump out of a deep arroyo, a greasewood branch got caught in his left saddlebag and ripped the seam out, spewing the contents back down the hill. It was late afternoon and Rider could see the end of the desert within a mile. A quick bit of sewing with some tie wire temporarily held the contents back in the pouch until the next real stop. Two trails converged next to some sheep corrals which Rider headed to.

It was mid afternoon and his ride through this first patch of real desert was finished. That he made it through rather comfortably instilled a dose of confidence in him for the next patch. Before he started his journey, he feared crossing deserts more than anything, mostly because he had never seen one until he stepped in one. In these corrals there was running spring water, a decent amount of grass and some shade trees. Rider figured he would laze out the rest of the afternoon as well as the next to repair gear and recover well enough to tackle his next fear he had before he started. He was now in, and about to cross the Indian Nations.

20.

Zuni People

Maybe it was the anxiety Rider was unknowingly transferring through the saddle to Jelly's soul. Maybe it was the eruption of stress the 3yr old horse could no longer contain. Whatever it was certainly grabbed a solid hold of the horse at an inopportune time, as if there is ever an opportune time.

Four hundred miles of poor feed, nasty water, strange smells and a pronounced case of homesickness seemed to finally catch up with its' equine quarry. As Rider began saddling the morning after an entire days rest Jelly threw a tantrum for the ages. This was a farting, snorting and bucking extravaganza, one that any 10 year old child would be proud of. Letting it play out, Rider simply held onto the mecate and stayed out of flying hoof range. Jelly was wailing, "I am not going any further", while Rider was whispering, "Wanna bet?" Once played out and standing full of sweat, Rider approached Jelly's nose and tucked it under his arm as always, and stroked his neck. Jelly was still in a snit so Rider began to lunge him in a circle just to get his mind right. Jelly was physically healthy and had regained some weight from the early days of the journey. Jelly's snit was hanging on so Rider kept the lunge going as if to drill a hole for water. When Jelly's ears finally told Rider that complete attention was being paid, the saddling process again began. The pecking order of man before beast now firmly reestablished, Rider mounted and after a few more tight circles, stepped out toward the corral gate, only to stare into the eyes of two men leaning on a rail. Rider had been so caught up in bringing Jelly back to reality that he left himself completely vulnerable to the surroundings. Neither of the men, obviously Indian, showed any hostility or desire to pull their revolvers from their holsters, so Rider folded his hands on the pommel and walked Jelly over to the men to say hello.

Richard Waikaniwa and his uncle wondered aloud if they were in a time warp, staring at a lone buckskin clad white man on his horse in the middle of the Zuni Indian Reservation. This likely had not been seen for more than 100 years.

Introductions made, Rider unsaddled Jelly and stowed his gear in the corner of the corral, as he knew it was likely polite to set awhile with these two gents; seeing as how he was in their lands. The gents just happened to have some fresh hay in their 30yr old pickup and the uncle carried a few flakes over to Jelly, and then wandered over to a shack a few hundred yards away. Richard motioned for Rider to stay where he was until he returned. Neither man spoke each others' native tongue but the snort of whiskey Rider provided bridged the language gulf as well as any lingering ancestral dislike for each others' people. Rider had no preconceived dislike for the Zuni; hell, he had never heard of the tribe, but the Zuni shared no affection for whites, as learned later.

Western Indians were the original slave traders in America. Zuni hated Navaho, Navaho hated Utes, Utes hated Shoshone and vice versa and so on amongst differing tribes. Anglos were the worst of the lot when finally showing up a few centuries ago.

Anglos were simply better equipped at slavery and war, after having learned the practice well back in their European homelands. Anglos were well versed in the art of mass killing and were continually and substantially more technologically advanced through the ages. Anglos fought with steel, armor and eventually guns, while the natives fought with sticks, leather and arrows. By the time American Indians acquired horses, the Anglos already had cannons. Additionally, the great expansive land mass of America prevented the actual 'learning' about war because of the great distance required to travel for the purpose of having a fight. This separation would prove to be a primary reason for eventual effective extermination of Indian Tribes because they were not geographically close enough to organize and join forces to battle the common Anglo foe.

Richard returned just after lunch with his niece, pressed into service as a translator. Richard was a part-time sheep herder and was a well respected elder of the Zuni. It was inferred that he had communicated to others that Rider was on the 'rez' and would be passing through. The uncle never reappeared. After weeks of being told by most to beware of riding thru the 'Nations', Rider came to learn that Richard was as kind a person he could ever hope to meet. After checking on Jelly, Rider climbed into the pickup and was treated to an impromptu expansive and moderated tour of the Zuni Nation. After a brief stop at Richard's house, Richard got back in the truck and the three drove around the reservation for a couple hours. He showed Rider places of significance to the Zuni, be it religious, sacred or places of great sorrow. Rider was introduced to family and friends along the way, all the while freely discussing the realities of reservation life and ills, as portrayed to outsiders. The excursion concluded back at Richard's home where Rider found himself in the company of all of the folks they had previously met, plus a whole bunch more.

The reservation telegraph, (aka word of mouth), had been quite busy and as Rider would soon learn in the coming days and weeks, said telegraph knew no borders in the Nations.

Richard's wife and pals had conjured up a huge pot of stew and Rider was motioned to dig in first and after doing so the feast began. Rider was peppered with questions while taking his first spoonful and it was delicious...until the hot peppers kicked in. Not wishing to be rude Rider struggled mightily to mask his discomfort with the spicy concoction to the point of watery eyes, he was finally rescued with a tall glass of water much to the comedic delight of the crowd. Despite numerous kind invitations for safer accommodations, Rider was returned to his horse where he could bed down beneath the stars in peace.

The prevailing Zuni religion is embedded in secrecy as it is with most native beliefs; especially when queried by outsiders. This is as it should be. Religion, language and blood relations are the true remaining bonds for these ancestral peoples. Outsiders in their zeal to be included where they don't belong only serve to threaten and pollute whatever threads of remaining heritage.

Rider was invited to a Kiva, a room for religious ceremony, but respectfully declined for this same reason. As Rider would plod through the Nations in the coming days he would be struck by his own sadness of witnessing the lives of a dying people. The ever present garbage and houses made of mud and straw called Hogans, each with a TV satellite dish affixed to it betold Rider of the lost pride of what once was. Years ago they must have suspected in their hearts when gazing into the first blue eyes they had ever seen, the end was beginning. It seemed that only now that the wise one's are finally recognizing the sadness of a heritage lost.

Rider rode with a ready smile and a worried heart for the kind people who would escort him through their lands, albeit from a distance. He now knew he would be safe in the Nations, all of them. The 'toktok', or Indian telegraph would be buzzing in all the

Nations all the way to the Nez Perce up near his home. All would know him, his spirit and 'medicine', and that this was how he would be safe from human harm. No tribe wanted to be known as the land where Rider perished on his journey. That's how the Nations worked. The next 60 miles through Zuni land was uneventful though Rider often saw people at a distance, he spoke to no one. Three days later he spied Gallup, New Mexico and the southern border of the massive 27,000 square mile Navaho Nation.

21.

Drunk Town

Gallup, New Mexico began as a railroad town in the late 1800's. It was a supply depot for railroad construction and soon became known as the 'Heart of Indian Country' due to its proximity to many tribal communities. The area also hosted the filming of many movies in the western genre in the 1940-1970 period.

It is also known as 'Drunk Town'.

At the southern edge of town Rider found a small ranch with a barn and paid to stable Jelly and then walked into town to find a room for a sound sleep. Jelly was going to receive extra rations of oats and Rider planned to give himself extra rations of sleep, fresh vegetables, bread and whiskey. He thought of finding a woman to rent but then decided against it; having the clap in the middle of nowhere was a powerful dissuasion.

It was also time for a decision, the first of its' kind. Keep heading north or start angling northwest. If he kept heading north he'd have safe travel in the high plains of Colorado but then would have to pass west through grizzly bear country. In addition he'd exit Navaho land near Farmington, New Mexico-a town that he had heard that Indian relations with white men had recently been ugly. If he started angling northwest, a more direct route home, he would pass through country heavily dotted with impassible canyons that could turn a traveler in circles for days on end. This decision was what Rider intended to think on while remaining as horizontal as possible for the next few days.

Border towns like Gallup are locales where Indian and white cultures meet for the purpose of tolerating each others' existence. From all over the reservation Indians come to cash their government allotment checks and sell their jewelry, blankets and other hand-made wares to the white merchants who gladly purchase the goods at 10% of the retail price they charge in their stores. All the while the merchants strive to convince the Indian of the enormous favor they do for their 'brother' by purchasing same. Rider spent idle time smoking cigars outside these pawn shop stores watching the trade take place. Most of the Indians Rider saw coming out of these shops were drunk within an hour of their windfall. Alcohol consumption is an art form in a border town, and drinking to obliteration is too frequently the achieved goal. Once the windfall is spent, personal items are pawned while hung-over and the return home is accomplished by hitching a ride in the back of pickups or dung strewed stock trailers. Three weeks later the process is repeated.

After a couple days of watching this scenario repeatedly play out, and becoming increasingly disgusted by it, Rider cut his mini vacation short, collected Jelly and headed out of town in the middle of the night. As with all towns he had to get through, walking his horse through town well after last call was the safest choice. Once through town, Rider chose the northwest direction and within a few miles learned that he was relegated to riding along the side of the road, as all gates and fences were well locked and secured. With so much drunkenness, theft and destruction was rampant. Even fence posts weren't safe as the drunks would light the creosote posts on fire so they could pass out with some heat.

Rider was told to head toward Window Rock, Arizona and once through that small town, things would open up again. He camped with Window Rock in sight the first night out of Gallup. The 35 miles passed like non-existent winds as Jelly was literally feeling his oats after a couple days of rich feed. Rider loosened the reins and gave Jelly his head as there was nowhere else to go other than the side of the road between the two towns. A lone white horseman clad in fringed buckskins in the nations created quite a curiosity for those passing by. Rider hated to be so close to cars and on an actual road, but there was nowhere else to ride.

The next morning found Jelly tied to a signpost outside a café in town, and the locals already knew who he was and what he was doing. The Navaho waitress that cleared his plates after breakfast told him that his meal had already been paid for, and this embarrassed Rider greatly; he was used to paying his own freight. As he stood and gathered his hat Rider said aloud that buying his meal was very kind and offered his thanks to whoever did so. A large Indian gent at a table with other workmen spoke up and said, 'We all did'. After a few minutes of toktok, Rider untied Jelly and walked the horse through the small town. As he walked people stopped their cars and got out to offer him sandwiches, money, drinks and one fellow took off his shirt and insisted Rider accept the offering. Rider never broke stride but was friendly and respectful yet uncomfortable with all the attention; he just wanted to get out of town and back on the trail. Most simply wanted to touch him, his spirit, and in that manner perhaps share the journey in their heart. There are many interpretations for this conduct; that of 'counting coup' or the touching of a perceived greater spirit in the hopes that by doing so enriches their own.

At one point Rider and Jelly passed a small elementary school during recess. It then took Rider about an hour to travel 100 yards. Waves of schoolchildren rushed across the street and flocked around man and horse much to the consternation of the teachers frantically trying to hold traffic and children at the same time. Seeing this play out, Rider walked Jelly across the street into the schoolyard apologizing to the teachers while calming Jelly. The schoolmarms were all smiling as they relented and recognized how uncomfortable Rider was being surrounded by a horde of wide-eyed and smiling little children. Traffic had slowed to a crawl, the school principal had joined in and the stir commenced in all its glory. Rider finally got everyone's attention and asked everyone to sit in front of him in a half circle because Jelly had never seen small humans and he did not want anyone to get hurt. The principal, a calm and beautiful Navaho gal in her mid-thirties with flowing black hair welcomed the horse and Rider and told him that everyone had heard of him, but never expected to see him. Rider answered countless questions about where he came from, why he was doing such a journey, and how he found food. Most of the questions however, were about the majestic Jelly. Toward the end of the impromptu session, Rider drew a map in the sand of the United States, complete with a quiz identifying each State, and outlined where he started and hoped to end up.

He was trying to gently extricate himself from the collection of kids after an appropriate time, and thankfully a pre-programmed school bell rang and goodbye's and lotsa leg hugging commenced as Rider led Jelly off the grounds. Rider was kind of energized by the experience but was mostly thankful that Jelly's first experience with little humans went well.

A couple miles north of town the locked gates and impenetrable fences disappeared and melded into open desert. Rider crossed to the west side of the road and headed north again in open country with a pronounced exhale of relief that his interaction with towns was likely over for many weeks to come.

It was the last day of April and Rider had covered 700 miles in a little more than six weeks. With a third of the journey completed, both horse and human were muscled up and healthy.

22.

Getting the Jump

Passing Fort Defiance, Arizona in the distance Rider cut into the open desert a few hours before dusk. He wanted to avoid towns for a while.   In the mid 1800's just before the Civil War, Fort Defiance was the site of some of the most despicable conduct the US Government ever directed toward native peoples. Untold numbers of Indians were exterminated or collected and cruelly interred at another regional Army post. The only reason that this mass genocide wasn't more horrific was that the Army abandoned the post at the outbreak of the war in the east. The place has been bad medicine ever since according to many locals. Rider was told that the next guaranteed water was the San Juan River on the other side of 250 miles of barren desert. The days were hot but not blistering. After a few days and with the moon heading to full, Rider decided to travel at night and hole up during the day. He figured that he could predict the moon better than he could predict the heat, cloudy conditions being the unknown. With the light colored sand and surrounding canyon walls, moonlight was enhanced by multiple reflective angles and was easy to see by. 250 miles of desert might take 3 weeks and if he met trouble, he wanted Jelly to be in the best shape possible. Travelling in the cool night air would help that cause. Toward evening Rider emerged out of some cut-bank hills into a small valley where he halted and watched a young Navaho boy astride a small paint pony that he was working the hell out of. The boy was desperately trying to herd about 50 head of thirsty cattle away from a stock tank for some reason.

'Ben', as Rider would later learn, was 12 winters old and stopped dead in his tracks when he finally noticed the bearded, buckskin clad white man setting on a magnificent horse watching him. The man and boy locked eyes from a distance of about 50 yards and both sat motionless. Rider sensed that the boy was disgusted with himself for letting someone easily get the jump on him-especially a white man. Rider raised his left hand to his chest, palm down and motioned it away from his body, and returned it to his reins while cracking a small smile. He turned Jelly aside and slowly walked him past the boy at a healthy and friendly distance seemingly paying the boy no further attention. If Ben was a grown man Rider would have approached directly but when dealing with a child Rider knew it was inappropriate to make contact and in the Indian culture very disrespectful. Peeking out of the corner of his eye, Rider noticed that Ben remained frozen, as if he was looking at a ghost. As Jelly slowly walked past the boy 'chaha'd the paint into a sudden gallop. Ten minutes later he heard the whining of an engine and saw a dust cloud rapidly approaching from behind a small rise. An old pickup soon materialized with the boy in the passenger seat, and Rider turned Jelly to face the truck and patiently collected his hands on the pommel. Stopping a few yards from Jelly the driver got out and said, 'Ho', to which Rider replied in kind. The man, who turned out to be Ben's father, motioned for his son to join him leaning on the front of the truck. Ben became translator as his father had no English, and Rider spoke no 'dine' or Navaho tongue.

Ben spoke when cued by his Dad, "You are the traveler we heard about"?

"Likely, name's Rider", Rider replied.

"I am Ben, my father does not speak yours".

"I understand", Rider said as he nodded respectfully to the man.

"Where are you going, Mister Rider?"

"I am heading to the Snake River country up in the State of Washington. I hope I didn't spook you Ben. I was admiring how you ride, but I couldn't figure out if you were working, practicing or playing! You are a very good horseman, young man."

Ben was translating all for his father. Like a kid caught with his hand in the proverbial jar, Ben replied, "It is fun. Where is Washington?"

"Far north, next to Canada."

"That is far", Ben said with disbelief. "You cannot get there, too many mesas".

"Well Ben I'll just have to figure that out through discovery, right? How far is the next water, do you or your father know?"

Ben and his father carried on a conversation in their 'dine' language and the father started to point out landmarks to Rider while speaking in what Rider could only make out as a series of grunts. Rider quickly wondered to himself that he must think my language is a series of grunts also! When the man finished Rider nodded in appreciation while realizing he didn't understand 'grunt' very well. Ben finally chirped up again and said that water is about 30 miles away, but if he followed the old wagon trail to the ruins of a Catholic mission in Lukachakai, he could shave 10 miles off the trip.

Goodbye's were said and since he had a full canteen and a moonlit night ahead Rider opted to try for the old mission road-mostly because he enjoyed saying 'Lu-catch-a-kai' aloud.

The mission road soon devolved into a sandy trail and never got any better. Rider often had to stop and study the surroundings to discern where the wind-blown sand had covered the trail. Soon he was navigating by rusty cans, old wagon parts, parched bits of leather and other remnants of travelers' past. After a few miles Rider could see the proverbial walls closing in. The mesa walls appeared to be more than 500' high and if it wasn't for the discarded remnants, Rider might have thought he was going into a boxed in canyon. The trail began to hug the eastern wall and in a few places small natural corrals were bored into the sandstone cliffs. These geological indentations were about 20' X 20' in size and full of lush vegetation and cool water seeping out of the rock wall. To collect the water from the rock face Rider placed a stick against the seep and angled it away from the wall and allowed it to collect into his hat. These small utopias were a godsend for weary travelers back in the day, just as they were for Rider in the present day. Although Rider was a growing a bit dubious about being directed into an apparent boxed in canyon, he knew there had to be an outlet based on the amount of trailside garbage.

Just about at the end of the canyon, Rider could see no obvious outlet, even though only 50 yards now separated the cliffs. He tied Jelly and went for a stroll to see the wall in front of him from different angles, hoping he would spy the exit, if there truly was one. The trail out began at an acute angle to the mission road and in its unused condition was very difficult to find.

He gathered Jelly and it took only 30 minutes to climb out of the canyon, as the trail was a winding, gentle pull. Easily wide enough for a wagon and team back in the day. Scanning his back trail, as he did religiously whenever he topped a rise, he could see how the canyon route was much more direct than had he kept to the more well used road, for looking north the ruins of the Lukachakai Mission was just ahead.

It was just past daybreak when Rider rode into the town that used to be Lukachakai. In addition to the church ruins there was a few weather beaten buildings remaining. There was an active stock tank at what had been the center of town, and this is where Jelly drank after Rider had drank his fill and washed up a bit. This ghost town was now simply a grazing stop, mostly for sheep. The town is an example of a town that 'almost was' in the early west, and likely would have persisted and grown had the white settlers been able to fight off the Indians with any success. The area is said to be of steep religious significance to Navaho and the Anasazi before them, and it was fiercely defended. The whites evidently decided that fighting another's' spooks wasn't worth the effort, so the black robes of the mission vacated either on foot, horseback or decomposed into the air.

There was a fair amount of green grass around the stock tank as it was obvious that it and the surrounding buildings had not been used by stock in quite some time. Rider hobbled Jelly and retired for the day in the shade alongside one of the buildings. He woke in mid afternoon long enough to take a leak and rub Jelly who had retired to the shade of a shed himself. Close to dusk they were back at it in the open desert, though this time without any knowledge of the desert ahead.

Riding into a desert without knowing where water can be found was an unsettling proposition, but Jelly was fresh and Rider's canteen was full, so off they went. Riding into mesa country also presented potential challenges, not because of the quicksand and critters there, but mostly that arroyos were indiscernible until you almost fell into them-and some were 100's of feet deep. He had a good moon and anytime there was a little rise he would point Jelly to the top so as to map out his northerly path and pick out any landmarks that might be available. The night was crisp and the sun woke up a lot sooner than Rider had thought it should, but it did. Just after dawn he stared into an arroyo and saw a flock of sheep followed by a horseman. He could hear the sheep bleating on the air and the herder seemed to be trying to bed the sheep to wait out the upcoming heat of the day. Rider could have easily skirted the arroyo undetected but assumed that the herder would likely see Jelly's tracks and start to investigate. So rather than try to fool the herder, he decided to get the jump on the fellow just to let him know that he meant no harm. Rider kept his distance but stepped Jelly close enough so that Rider spoke a loud, "Ho", the herder would surely hear. Though too far away to make out facial features the herdsman turned and looked at Rider. Rider motioned as he had with Ben, pointed north and waved goodbye. The herdsman also raised his hand and Rider moved off hoping that would be the end of the conversation. Neither man kept their attention on the other in an obvious manner, but both did.

Prior to dropping off into the arroyo Rider had already mapped his route out of it and his route beyond.

He also knew in his gut that the herdsman would not allow himself to let well enough alone, so he tried to figure a route that gave him more flank advantage than less. Not knowing the lay of the land was a great disadvantage but Rider hoped he could put enough ground between himself and the sheepman to make the issue moot. Reaching the canyon floor Rider decided that outrunning the gent was not an option so he decided to stop for a while to find out whether he was going to be trailed or not. In the backcountry it pays to be more careful than less. He tied Jelly to some desert shrubs around a bend and scrambled up the hill to set awhile and gaze at the spot he figured the sheepman would appear if he was going to. In about ten minutes his theory proved correct, as he could see the herder coming along holding his horse to a careful walk while reading the earth. He held his reins in his left hand while resting the butt of his rifle on his right thigh- he was being more careful than less also. Rider wanted to get the jump on the fellow, but not so much as to be construed as threatening, and so he did by again saying 'Ho', as soon as the herdsman got close enough for polite conversation. And polite conversation it was. Rider chose his spot well as the horse had just stepped up onto a small rise in the trail, leaving the herder at a disadvantage by having to lean forward too much to be immediately aggressive if that was his intent.

'Sammy' appeared to be in his early fifties and clearly recognized his disadvantage as well as being silently perturbed that he let Rider outsmart him. The two spoke easily despite not knowing much of the other's tongue. Sammy knew more English than Rider knew 'dine' by a long shot. Rider said that he was just passing through and Sammy could see that was so, after inspecting the gear lashed to Jelly from a short distance. Rider could tell from Sammy's mannerisms that the herdsman decided to take Rider as he was and let him be.

Sammy spoke of the same landmarks that Rider had picked out earlier from atop the mesa, which confirmed that Rider's choice of direction was well chosen. Sammy mentioned some water holes farther on but could not guarantee them given the current drought. This at least gave Rider some idea of where to angle to and was quite thankful for the information. Goodbyes were said and both parted after booting their rifles in their scabbards at about the same time. The first spring Sammy mentioned was located a couple hours later to the north and Rider walked Jelly a short distance away to make camp and sleep out the day. There was plentiful feed around the spring and with the moon now waning, Rider decided to wait til morning to set out again. He still had some crackers and cheese along with some sausage remaining in his kit so he was in good shape for a longer rest than usual.

23.

Spiders n' Spaniards

Rider got a very early start the next morning thanks to a curious Black Widow spider crawling up his arm seeking a warm place to sleep. It was about 3am when the spider entered that big web in the sky. Had Rider slapped at the spider in haste rather than waking calmly and allowing the spider to crawl on his other hand so he could set it on the ground-and then squish it-his bones might never have been found.

By noon Rider was leaning against a windmill that was pumping fresh water into an overflowing stock tank while appreciating life just a little more this day. Jelly was munching on some leftover alfalfa while Rider was pondering whether to head into the tiny town in the distance. Mexican Water, Arizona used to have a population and got its name from being the location of some natural water wells that dried up long ago, just like the population. It was getting hot and being in the middle of nowhere, Rider decided to strip down to his birthday suit and bathe for awhile in the stock tank. After a good soaking he lay naked on his blanket and let the sun and breeze be his towel. He spent the rest of the afternoon under a makeshift sunshade watching ants travel from one hole to another, and nowhere else. He considered that there was probably a parable between the ants and his journey, but for the life of him he couldn't figure out what it was.

Rider was enthralled with sunsets within the mesa walls. As the sun moved toward sleep, each angle highlighted the chameleon-like earth tones available to the eyes for only moments, until new sets of hues take their place. He was also watching his horse, for Jelly seemed a bit weary even while resting. The desert crossings had taken its cumulative toll on Jelly, and his hips were starting to show too much. All the up and down riding had begun to create 'hotspots' on his withers and back, the precursor to sores and fistulas. Rider continually rigged the cinch angles to try to avoid such sores, and was doing more walking than riding. He figured he had another 40-50 miles until he struck the San Juan River, where he intended to camp along the banks for more than a few days.

The next morning he set the saddle on snug, but too loose to ride. He figured he could lead Jelly most of the day, and ride only for a couple hours. Still picking his way among the sandstone monuments and mesas, he was relieved when seeing that the 'up down' country was beginning to slack off and flatten out. This would be easier on Jelly as well as his buffalo hide moccasins as he plodded along. Five centuries ago the Spanish Conquistadors gazed at the land ahead just like Rider was doing now-nothing has changed. The 'Old Spanish Trail', which Rider was following now, was nothing more than a wide swath in the desert; it wasn't like they, or he, had a choice in the matter. The Trail was basically a series of tentacles off what was a trade route in the mid 1800's between California and the interior of the country. This particular tentacle heading north into Utah still was occasionally churning up artifacts from that period. Many locals are said to have various and sundry 'conquistador' items on display in their homes. Attempting travel in a northerly direction anywhere but in this wide valley was close to impossible given the arroyos and mesas, so the Old Spanish Trail was to be Rider's trail for the foreseeable future.

Jelly was struggling a bit now and Rider seldom mounted up. Getting Jelly home safe and healthy, barring accident, was to be a measure of the quality of Riders' acumen as a horseman. The code of the west that to care for your horse before yourself was borne out of survival more than anything else, for being afoot in dangerous country was as good as being dead.

He led Jelly along all that night and the following day. Rider wasn't too concerned about navigation or finding water, and enough feed was found in sparse allotments along the way for Jelly. If travelers in years past had done it Rider could too. On the third afternoon the San Juan Valley was a mile away but with a 4000' decent in between. Smooth sandstone boulders provided stepping stones all the way down. Rider hobbled Jelly at the top and tied his headstall to his foreleg and descended to scout for a route down, wanting to be sure they could reach the valley once they started down.

Some of the jumps they would have to make on the way down were 'one-way' efforts, and Rider did not want to be stuck on a cliffside. It took an hour for Rider to return to Jelly, who hadn't moved much, which is what Rider had wanted to ensure by tying him in such a manner. Old timers would 'head hobble' their horse to its feet with the nose low for the same reason, but also to keep their animal from whinnying, as a horse can't muster up anything more than a snort with its nose down by his knees.

Back then a whinny could mean death from those astride other horses once an enemy was exposed by some horse looking for a little equine companionship. It took a couple hours and a few occasions of convincing to get Jelly to the valley floor. Some of the jumps Jelly had to make were over deep chasms and the footing on the sandstone was squirrely. Jelly was sweating hard due to stress, but going back up wasn't an option. Back when the journey started two months previous, Jelly would never have agreed to follow Rider down the cliff, but he now had a deep trust in the man who led him down the perilous path, although the horse would likely never agree to do it again.

24.

Bluffoonery

Jelly was hobbled on a small island in the middle of the San Juan River at noon the following day, munching on alfalfa and enjoying life in general. They had strolled into the small town of Bluff, Utah the previous evening and Rider arranged to purchase a couple bales of alfalfa, and some oats while having a wonderful meal at the local café. While tied to a hitching rail, Jelly received all the spoils that little kids and tourists showered on this 'real mountain man horse'. Jelly was in heaven and Rider not too far behind and after a wonderful meal he then supplied himself for the upcoming few days of rest and relaxation. He was also able to buy a pint of good whiskey from the hidden stock of the café owner. Utah was a dry State meaning hard liquor was hard to come by. Small shop owners in out-of-the-way locales often held hidden stocks of hooch to sell to trusted locals. Even though Rider wasn't a local, the storekeeper also knew he sure wasn't a Fed in disguise either, so he sold the bottle without worry.

Rider had spent the morning treating Jelly's hotspots on his back with mud and cool grasses. Jelly needed some serious rest, and Rider decided that hanging out in a well made shelter on the banks of the river only a ¼ mile from town was a good place to spend a week. The desert had challenged Jelly's spirit. He toughed it out but the effort had exhausted his reserves. Rider would not start out until Jelly was strong again.

The second day camped on the river was filled with horse care, swimming, sunbathing and taking meals at the local café. Word had travelled around this little burgh of 300 souls, the first Mormon settlement Rider would encounter, that a cross country traveler was in their community and during the second day quite a few locals wandered over to say hello. Even though the whole town obviously knew where he was camped, Rider felt secure. On the third morning Jelly again found himself hobbled on the island with alfalfa, shade and cool running water. The San Juan River runs fast and shallow. Jelly's island was separated from shore by 30' of river but only belly deep.

Rider stowed his gear and decided to explore the river with some new pals on a raft. The river meanders through the heart of Anasazi country, a people who seemingly dissolved into the canyon walls hundreds of years ago. Petroglyphs, pictographs and cliff dwellings dotted the canyons. The scenery was otherworldly.

After a full day of exploration, the raft stowed and goodbyes said, Rider wandered back to the café for a meal only to find a hobbled Jelly tied to the hitching post. Jelly nickered and seemed to say that his day had been one long fezzle. It was about 7pm when Rider wandered into the café knowing there would be a story to hear about. The café folks just couldn't wait to tell him of Jelly's day while Rider silently confirmed to himself that towns always invited trouble. Townsfolk had a mindset borne out of an existence on concrete, rubber and asphalt; common sense decreases in direct proportion to technological increases he always thought.

The story told was that along about mid afternoon Jelly decided to go for a walk back to the place where he had been so spoiled a couple days earlier. The horse evidently hobbled his way across the river, down a ¼ mile sandy wash, under a bridge, clamored up the arroyo hillside and crossed the two lane highway on his way back to the café expecting more goodies and fawning. An obese red headed female from North Carolina happened by the café with her equally overweight children and decided that since she was from North Carolina, home to pampered, shiny, inbred, knot headed race horses, she knew what all horses were supposed to look like-even though she had probably never seen a real work horse in her life. Seems this gal considered Jelly to be an abused animal and took it upon herself to contact the county sheriff. It also happened that an all-too-young Deputy passed by and 'yes ma'amed' his way into a frazzle. Adding to this confluence of idiocy was that in recent months many locals had reported sighting a three legged cougar, and in some quirk of congenital spasm, the young Deputy assumed that Jelly's owner must have been killed by same. By the time Rider appeared back on the scene, the young Deputy was in the midst of organizing a search and rescue mission, complete with air support, to locate the likely remains of the mysterious horseman they had all heard so much about.

The café crew told Rider that the young Deputy lived nearby and was in the process of excitedly organizing his 'backwoods gear' at present, so Rider wandered over to the young man's trailer. When Rider found the trailer he saw the Deputy in his yard dutifully organizing his kit while on the phone to his boss, the county Sheriff. The Deputy, half dressed in his gear, took a quick break from his conversation once realizing who Rider was and continued his phone conversation for a couple more minutes walking out of earshot of Rider. The Deputy came over to Rider and handed him the phone with the sheriff on the line. The Sheriff immediately began to harangue Rider about county expenditures, manpower and the control he exercised over 'his' county. He finished by 'ordering' Rider out of not only 'his' county, but also the entire State of Utah. Rider replied that he would be camped along the river until he felt ready not to, and invited the Sheriff to come and meet him in person. He then suggested to the Sheriff that he likely had larger issues to deal with than all those he had harangued about, especially if his police force was not capable to backtrack an unbloodied, hobbled horse a ¼ mile in sand. He suggested further that his assuming that a gent had met his demise at the paws of a mythical three legged cougar based on a hobbled horse standing in the doorway of a café was a case of buffoonery at its zenith, and handed the noisy phone back to the Deputy while he could still hear the Sheriff screaming as he strolled away.

Halfway back to the café Rider could still hear the Deputy shouting an expletive laced diatribe about arresting him and such. Rider grabbed a sandwich from the mirthful café crew and gathered Jelly's reins, removed the hobbles and headed back to his river campsite. Prior to leaving he mailed a short note to his friends up in Washington just in case the insulted Sheriff was too creative at conjuring up false charges. The next morning Rider wandered over to visit with his new rafting pals and they all strolled over to the café to chortle about county law enforcement and wonder about a new species of cougar.

25.

Chaaco

Rider had a decision to make. Jelly was strong again but the strength was not bone strong, as they say. He had learned that the next few hundred miles north the trail was through scrubby high desert terrain. He could expect lots of rocky hills with sparse feed and dry washes that in normal times were creeks and streams. Rider felt that Jelly could walk but not be ridden, so he decided to ask about any horses that might be for sale in the area. The café crew said they would put the word out and oh by the way the Sheriff had been by and left a message for Rider ordering him out of the county, again. Rider admitted to the crew that he was a tolerable horseman but even he could not make Jelly fly, so the Sheriff would simply have to understand that getting out of 'his' county might take a few days of walking. That afternoon a gent appeared at Rider's camp saying that he might have a couple horses for sale but he would have to clear it with his young children first.

Rider met the man at his home the next morning. His Navaho wife knew a bit of English and the children were wary. Chaaco was their favorite horse. She was jet black with one white hoof and her entire training consisted of the kids being placed on her back while Dad led them around their corral. She had been blanketed but never saddled. The horse was extremely head wary, not shy, likely due to someone beating the crap out of her face in frustration or meanness in general.

Out of the four horses in the corral, Chaaco was the only horse with enough bottom in her to make a trail, like the one Rider was facing, so Rider made an offer for about ½ the asking price. Rider returned to the river and decided that this camp suited him just fine and he would lounge around for a couple more days. The following afternoon the gent reappeared and the deal to purchase

Chaaco was made. Rider spent the next two days in the family corral putting some training on his new horse, in full view of the Navaho gal and the wary kids.

He got Chaaco to the point of accepting a saddle, bosal and eventually a man on her back without continual mild bucking. Chaaco would squaw rein, meaning that the horse would go in the direction her nose was pulled, as opposed to moving out away from pressure, and in the backcountry that was enough for Rider. At dawn the next morning Rider led both horses out of town and into what was known as Cottonwood Wash, but now smirkingly named by the Café crew as '3 Legged Cougar Wash', whenever the Deputy or Sheriff happened by.

Once out of sight, Rider tied Jelly's mecate to Chaaco's tail and led them both off. Rider had spent eight days in Bluff, and thoroughly enjoyed all of them-a pleasant place to breathe a life. Rider was told that the wash, or dry creek bed, would eventually turn into an impenetrable maze of arroyos filled with pockets of quicksand. Rider chose to ride the wash rather than follow the road north to Blanding. The wash was sandy terrain and astride a new horse given to bucking, Rider figured sand was a softer to land on than asphalt. Both horses were getting acquainted on the trail, and sorting out the pecking order.

Rider should have given the horses another day in the corral by themselves for this purpose, but he was ready to move on. Now on the trail Rider rode Chaaco and dallied Jelly's mecate onto a makeshift saddle ring. If Jelly got too close to Chaaco's butt, he'd have to quickly avoid a flying hoof or two, so pretty soon he did not want to follow at all. All this going on while Rider was trying to keep his seat on Chaaco's back. He considered some options to the horse leading predicament. The first option was that Rider untied the bosal reins from Jelly's headstall and lengthened the mecate. This worked fine for a while but gave more elasticity to the tie rope, so when Jelly did not keep pace, Rider's saddle would be pulled back under Chaaco and bucking commenced. The next option was tying Jelly's lead rope to Chaaco's tail and this was functioning well until the first ditch needed to be jumped. Chaaco liked to jump while Jelly liked to step across. Chaaco's tail hair kept getting shorter and shorter with this option because her tail hair kept getting ripped out. The more that Jelly wasn't paying attention, the shorter the tail got and the madder Chaaco got.

Chaaco had a comfortable pace of 5-6 miles per hour, and Jelly's comfortable pace was about 3-4 miles per hour. Jelly could be the lead horse for Chaaco, but Chaaco would keep running into his butt and a frenzy would likely ensue. Additionally Jelly could not be ridden because of the soft condition of his back. Rider finally settled on the option of that he finally dismounted and led Jelly with Chaaco tied to his tail. Over time both horses would reach a tolerable compromise, but during the process Rider preferred to be walking on terra firma rather than landing on it.

Among Chaaco's quirks was her great fear of being trapped in quicksand. She still was very head sensitive even shying away from gentle strokes on her face. And if Rider held up a coiled rope she would blink and turn her head away expressively. It was clear that her head shyness was due to someone whipping her face in her past, and just as obvious was that she had been caught in quicksand at some point before. Every time her hooves sank even a little bit she 'crow-hopped', or jumped to the side as if a rattlesnake was in her path. If Rider was mounted on her, he could never relax because of this.

It took the outfit an exasperating two days to travel 40 miles to Blanding, Utah. Rider had learned of a veterinarian in that town and he wanted Jelly to get checked out.

26.

The Last War

Blanding's vet, a generous bear of a man named Clyde Watkins was in the process of constructing a large log cabin to house his wife Joanne and their collective brood, when Rider rode in. There were kids everywhere and the large barn and half finished house screamed love and home. In exchange for Dr. Watkins care for Jelly, Rider installed the plumbing in the new home. Rider bedded down in the barn and on the afternoon of the third day, the results of drinking crappy desert water finally caught up with him, and he fell very ill. He spent 3 days recovering in the hay with nasty stomach issues but finally began to rehydrate and gain his strength. On the eighth day of his stay he finished his work on the house, and Dr. Watkins invited Rider to lunch on the 'morrow and asked him to ride Jelly to the lunch spot.

There was quite a crowd in a field next to a ditch when Rider rode up to the lunch spot the next day, as per Dr. Watkins directions. After a hearty dutch oven meal one of the older gents stood up and welcomed Rider to the community and asked if he would join some of the men in a short horseback ride along the 'posse trail' that only a few locals knew about. About 10 older gents mounted up and while doing so, informed Rider that they were all using their fathers' saddles. It seems that in 1923 the "Last Indian War in the US", was fought near Blanding and all of these gents fathers' had been on the posse back then when hunting the renegade Chief Posey.

A common happening back then was that Indian Chief's were usually doing their best to retain their peoples' independence by not moving to reservations and Chief Posey was no different. The pressure for grazing land ownership by the whites was squeezing all Indians to do so.

This particular conflict ended when the 60 something year old Chief was shot above the hip and met his maker after 6 days of suffering up in a cave on Comb Ridge. The story goes that the old Chief would light a smoky fire every night so his captured people sequestered back in town would keep their spirit up by knowing the Chief was still alive. On the sixth night of the vigil there was no smoke and the posse felt safe enough to leave their outflanked position and go and confirm what was obviously a hideous and painful death; lying in the desert heat dying of blood poisoning.

Now 70 years later the sons of the posse members were leading Rider along the same trail the posse followed and at different spots each old gent stopped and told a story handed down from their fathers about that fateful day. After an hour the last gent stopped at the foot of Comb Ridge- an 80 mile long wall, to tell his story. At the end of his story he pointed out a rock ledge from which he said that Chief Posey had shot at his Dad and almost killed his son-the son being the very same old gent telling the story. As the other old gents smiled, this confused Rider, for how could the elderly gent currently telling the story at present-be killed by Posey's bullet more than 70 years ago? As Rider began to ask the question the old gent lifted his left leg out of his stirrup and pointed to a bullet hole where his crotch, and his Dad's long ago, was.

Another inch and the bullet would have blown off Dad's balls, and hence the old feller telling the story would have never been born.

27.

Getting' er Done

Before Rider started his journey he knew he would have a few seemingly insurmountable obstacles to cross, the Colorado River and National Highways among them. In the next week or so, he would be facing the Colorado and then soon after the first substantial National Highway. Back in Gallup crossing Highway 40 had been a breeze, but in comparison to the upcoming Highway 70, 40 was a much less traveled pipsqueak.

The next 200 miles would be a process of keeping the

road, Rt 191, at a comfortable distance. The vast majority of highways on the planet were first paths, then trails, then roads and finally highways. All took the path of least resistance and expense to get somewhere. In this high desert, roads followed alongside substantial cliffs and arroyos and keeping away from towns and roads was a challenge for Rider and his new found string. He crossed a bridge over the Colorado just north of Moab, Utah in the middle of a cool night with nary a vehicle in sight. Not only was this worrisome obstacle solved but while camping a mile north of same, he welcomed and relished the first raindrop he felt since his journey began, 77 days prior.

Two days of solid riding followed the last four since leaving Blanding, and both horses were in a routine by this time. He reached the old railroad siding Crescent Junction, Utah, just after noon and found a garden hose at the small station. There he learned that Chaaco liked to swallow the hose rather than drink from it, probably a learned skill from the little kids she grew up with. Rider grabbed a couple candy bars from a vending machine and the string walked across Highway 70 in between just a few cars. He wanted to keep a northern track but he was staring at the formidable Book Cliffs 20 miles in the distance. The Book Cliffs are an 800 mile wall in the high desert and getting through them was not an option. About a mile north of the junction was a dirt road heading west so Rider opted for unimpeded travel for a change. He switched saddles to Chaaco to put some more training on her and more miles under saddle. She was beginning to neck and knee rein and everyone was getting along better after a week of solid riding. They had really gotten it done the last week, traveling almost 150 miles. Another short day of travel and they would rest along the banks of the Green River, or Seeskadee as the old fur trading mountain men had called it.

Rider could see pine tree covered mountains in the distance and knew he had survived the deserts, even though there was another 100 miles of it left to go.

He was now approaching terrain he was more accustomed to, being an expert in living in mountain terrain versus being a neophyte in the desert. He could almost smell the trees.

28.

The Last Desert

He got to Green River and never broke stride as he rode Chaaco with Jelly's mecate dallied in his right hand right into the river. The first major river crossing went off without a hitch and he skirted the town without giving stopping a thought. He immediately angled northwest following the foothills on his right with a road and lava beds a couple miles to the left. The valley he was riding in was dotted with 12' arroyos so pronounced that they were almost undetectable until right on top of them. There was always a narrow game trail angling in and out of these land cavities so getting past them was no great challenge. Chaaco was now stepping rather than jumping ditches much to the relief of Jelly, who was being almost exclusively led at this point. It had been more than a week since Chaaco's hooves had connected with Jelly's face. As the valley narrowed Rider could see another river ahead and beyond an apparition of a small truck stop along the road. It was still daylight when Rider made camp along the Price River, choosing not to cross the horses so they would not be cold and wet all night. His own hide he cared little, so he stripped down and carried his clothes above his head as he waded across in hopes that the café was still open at the truck stop, which it was. After a ham sandwich he bought a bag of pretzels and a quart of beer, jumped in the back of a pickup truck and was dropped off on the bridge that crossed the river a half mile away.

A short stroll back to his horses and a pleasant evening was had by all.

The next morning Rider saddled up as usual and crossed the Price River. He wandered into a stand of cottonwood trees amongst green grass along the river's edge. He spent a couple hours fashioning a corral from downed trees, thanks to the resident beavers, and that was the extent of the work all would do for the day. He had stumbled into the ghost town of Woodside, Utah, home to a clear water geyser that resulted from a well dug by the expanding railroad in the late 1800's. A small town soon grew around this railroad water stop and a few years later Butch Cassidy used the town as a hideout. As trains got more technologically advanced the requirement for multiple water stops diminished and so did the towns that housed them. Rider had a wonderful day exploring the old ranch houses that were still standing and tried to figure out why the town was laid out as it was. He was back in the café well before closing time so the kitchen was open for a great burger and milkshake. When he was able to latch on to some milk he did so with glee.

Keeping along the east bank of the river until the lava beds joined in, Rider spent the next two days mostly leading his horses. He always tried to time his arrivals and passages through towns so he could get through them first, then camp and walk back if he so chose. At dusk on the second day he could see the lights of Price, Utah and decided to make camp along the river and be up and moving well before dawn so he could skirt town to the east. He drank a lot of water so as to set his pee alarm clock. It was about 7am when Rider found an old section of dirt road against a cliff that the railroad had mostly covered over with a 15' tall riprap railroad bed, forming a natural corral about as big as a football field. Both horses seemed out of sorts on this morning and Jelly's color inside his mouth was almost white, instead of its usual healthy red. By now the feed store he had seen while passing through town would be open so he hobbled the horses and

100

strolled to it to buy some good feed for his steeds. He strolled into the old feed store, complete with creaky wooden floors, in his fringed buckskin pants and a long underwear styled green shirt. His battered brown leather hat rested on his barely haired head and a scruffy red beard. An old fellow behind the counter looked up and asked if Rider had just come out of the last century, and once learning of Riders' journey, allowed he must have. He proceeded to grab a couple of used rubber buckets, cut open a bag of "COB", (corn, oats and bran), tossed a small aluminum stock tank in the back of a company owned pickup and filled it with water as he said, "We'll go slow". While chatting Rider spied an old set of spider web covered soft panniers hanging on the wall in the feed shed, suitcases for horses, and wondered if they'd be for sale.

They got tossed in the back of the pickup also while Rider was told that his money wasn't any good. With the horses extremely well fed but still a little wan, Rider left them to buy supplies, now that he had additional room to carry same. He found a small grocery store and chose all the foods he hadn't had space to carry the first 90 days of the journey. He was also able to purchase a small jar of hooch at a barbershop down the street; much in the same manner as back in the prohibition days.

Rider fashioned a lean-to against the cliff and ate, napped and watched his horses graze. He decided that he would see how his horses were feeling later in the day before deciding when to hit the trail again. He would be heading into the beginnings of what the mountain men used to call the High Lonesome, as the snow capped mountains he would have to cross were to the north and west of him. The month of June was a good time to travel in the mountains for the grass was sprouting, water was plentiful, undergrowth was at a minimum and little critters could be had for food. It made no sense to kill a full grown animal like a deer and waste most of it, when a fawn could be eaten for two or three days on the trail.

Just before dawn a terrible scream thrust Rider to consciousness. On the railroad tracks Chaaco was frozen in fear as Jelly had somehow managed to hobble down the riprap boulders that made up the railroad bed. The two horses had developed a relationship dynamic in which Chaaco would not leave Jelly, but Jelly seemingly could care less about Chaaco. This might have had to do with Chaaco kicking Jelly so often in the first week they knew each other, Rider thought in good humor. When it was light enough for Chaaco to see, she learned that Jelly had wandered off and she couldn't see him, and that scared her greatly. Rider began to slip on his moccasins when he heard a train whistle off in the distance, and that brought him to a dead run toward Chaaco. He scrambled up the rocks and was able to grab Chacco's halter just as he saw the train appear around the bend. He untied his rope belt, looped it around the halter and jumped off the railroad bed hoping his belt would hold. The horse was forced to also jump because of the weight Rider's jump forced on her head. Rider, still in his wool socks, could feel Chaaco right behind him.

As soon as Rider found purchase he jumped to the side hoping he wouldn't get trampled by the scared 1000 pound animal also trying to find some footing. No harm done other than a rude awakening so Rider stripped off his sweaty clothes, flopped back into his nest and slept for another three hours.

It was an overcast day and Rider led the horses along railroad bed to Helper, Utah, completing the 20 mile jaunt just at dusk. Helper was so named for the additional train engines required to help pull heavy freight trains up a 15 mile grade to Soldier Summit, Utah, back in the mining days. It was also a favorite Butch Cassidy haunt back in the day. Late morning the next day the string arrived in the ghost town of Colton, Utah, one of the many ghost towns found in what was becoming mining country. There were still a few standing buildings on the town site and Rider wandered around for a bit as the horse's grazed while

still saddled. They made Soldier Summit just before dusk.
Throughout the journey Rider had noticed that towns or the
remnants of same were consistently a one day horse ride apart,
while along popular byways. Some of these byways had evolved
into actual roads while most gave way to more efficient paths. He
wished he would have known that prior to starting out back on
Cloverdale, for he might not have been so nervous about his trail
to begin with. The factoid was now moot as he was about to cut
into the mountains completely void of civilization. After three
months of desert, the still snow covered Wasatch Mountains
loomed an hours' ride away, and he was unsure of Chaaco, for
she had never seen snow.

29.

Cabin Life

Traveling at a consistent 6000' elevation in springtime in
the mountains is as good as it gets. All the smells are fresh and
new, as plants wake up and struggle for sun. Two days after
heading into the mountains Rider happened upon the ghost town
of Willow Creek, Utah. All that remains are some foundations and
sealed off mines. The US Forest Service maintains a guard
station with a ½ acres fenced corral for their riding stock when
they visit. The guard station was a small cabin with a nail stuck in
the door hasp so the wind, bears or snow drifts wouldn't force the
door open, but people in need of emergency shelter could. It was
too early in the spring for Forest Service visits so Rider had
himself righteous accommodations for a couple days while the
horses got acclimated to the chilly nights and grew out their hair a
bit. Rider spent the first couple hours putting the barbed wire
fence back up, as one of the last tasks in the fall was to lay the
fence down so the weight of the snow wouldn't crush it. Lush

green grass was already springing up in this verdant valley where Indians and mountain men used to gather for 'rendezvous' back in the fur trapping days. The soft panniers were full from the Soldier Summit store and Rider spent the next two nights sleeping soundly on the bed frame, in between killing mice. The cupboards had some canned beans that Rider made good use of and at one point saw a large Bull Moose trot across the field in front of the horses, not paying them any mind.

While the horses farted, rolled and generally enjoyed their healthy enclosure, Rider poked around the old town site and found numerous old mine entrances and rusty remnants of that time. It always amazed him how nature eventually always took over, reclaimed and prevailed over land once borrowed by humans. He did not find a cemetery which was unusual after recreating the town site in his mind. In all these ghost towns, finding the site of a livery or blacksmith shop was always the easiest due to the amount of discarded metal remnants, and there always was a cemetery. Cemeteries were usually the most vital source of information about a town's life and death, for the birth and death dates on the headstones provided a reference for when that particular town was most active. Rider was disappointed that he wasn't able to locate one at this site. On the third morning Rider started north and it just so happened that a forest service trail was heading the same direction. Abundant feed and water and no bear sign yet found, made the next two days highly enjoyable. Setting a horse with nothing but the sweet smelling mountain breeze swishing through the pine trees brought Rider to wonder about his life and why he was the kind that always needed to see what was around the next bend, but also somewhat cursed to always have to. The old mountain men always considered themselves smarter than most civilized folk in that up in the mountains there was ample time to think about life and such, where in town too much time was dedicated to interacting with other folks about insignificant blather. In the mountains a fellow could really 'ponder' in earnest and without interruption.

In the crisp afternoon late in the day, Rider was astride Chaaco on a cliff overlooking a huge deep blue body of water nestled in a lush green alley about 2000' below. He immediately knew that his diet would enjoy a bit of a change because fish would be his next meal.

30.

Old Tom

Mid afternoon found Rider astride Jelly walking down the gravel road that hugs the western shore of Strawberry Reservoir. The reservoir was constructed in the early 1900's to provide irrigation for a large portion of central Utah, as well as now being one of the premier recreational fisheries in the west. The Strawberry valley was surrounded by lush green foothills flowing down to the deep blue reservoir waters. Dotted along the transition areas of where the green grass met the tall pine trees and cottonwoods were a few of the remaining cabins that belonged to the now submerged ghost town of the same name.

While riding along, an old yellow Ford pickup pulled alongside and the cowboy driving hollered out, "You're travelin?"-more of a statement than a question.

Rider nodded and the old cowboy, wearing a sweat stained white straw cowboy hat again shouted, "Left rear leg of your horse is gimpy, at the end of this road cross over the highway and put your mounts in the corral in back", and drove off without waiting for a response.

This time it was more of an order than a statement. Rider smiled a bit and kept walking Jelly along. Seeing it was coming night time soon anyway, and the promise of a corral in which he wouldn't have to hobble his horses, he figured to do as the old man had commanded.

Tommy Farrar was 73 years old and was Lord and Master of his world, which included his wife of the same age, Gladys.

They had been married for over fifty years, and she addressed him as Old Tom, as she had since the day they were married. Tom had been a cowboy for the nearby Mormon Ward his whole life-it was his first and only job. Single handedly he rode herd on twelve hundred head of pregnant cows from spring to fall. In early spring the cattle would arrive and it was Tom's job to manage the range and keep track of calves as they came. There were about eighty owners of the herd and Tom single handedly kept track of which cows belonged to which owners.

Back in the pioneer days when the nearby Heber City was being organized, small irrigation canals were built with manually manipulated diversion planks that allowed each family a defined amount of time to receive irrigation water for their personal vegetable gardens based on the number of cattle they owned. The more cows a family owned, the longer they could receive water for their gardens. When water was scarce this was a well organized solution to a potentially unneighborly problem. The system remains in force but with the augmentation of Strawberry Reservoir, it is not as closely monitored as it once was.

Tom was up at first light every day, and rarely stayed awake past 9pm. His whole life was regimented and orderly, unless he was in the saddle, then he was free as a bird. Rider was brushing his horses when Tom strode over on a pair of bowlegged legs that reflected a lifetime of riding barrel chested horses. They shook hands and introduced themselves and Tom stated that the horses needed a rest before attempting to cross over the High Uinta Mountains to the north and that the pass was likely still snowed in.

He told Rider that Gladys had dinner waiting for both of them and that Rider would start working for Tom in the morning at

$10 per hour cash money. He told Rider to stow his gear in the shed and that is where he was to sleep, and that he'd holler for Rider in the morning when breakfast was ready. Tom turned on his heel and walked back to the red shingled house that had sheltered him and his wife for the past fifty years or so.

By this time Rider could barely stifle a giggle at the situation he had walked into. He stowed his gear as instructed and strolled over to the house where Gladys met him at the screen door with a sincere welcoming smile and pointed to a chair at the kitchen table.

"Are you gonna say the prayer Rider", Tom loudly stated while staring down Rider with his aged, but clear blue eyes.

Rider held the stare for a longer moment than necessary and spoke to Gladys while still holding Tom's eyes, "Maam, please don't take offense but I don't cotton for religion much so it would be disrespectful if I were to make it seem that I did by saying a prayer to whatever apparition you folks choose to subscribe by. I'll just thank you kindly for your kindness and take my leave if you wish."

Gladys smiled and patted Rider's hand and Tom bellowed, "We don't believe in that bullshit either, sorry Mother, let's eat."

At 6am sharp the next morning Rider heard Tom bellow from across the dirt and gravel yard, "Breakfast", and Rider joined Tom at the table while Gladys washed some dishes.

"We'll go build some fence this morning and then we'll go to Heber for supplies. We'll need the small chainsaw and the gas can, the barbed wire is already in the back of the truck."

Rider nodded and finished his meal and started to collect his utensils, cup and plate to bring to the sink but Tom bellowed, "That's her job."

Rider paid him no mind and said to Gladys while eyeing Tom with a smile, "Is he always this ornery or did I catch him on one of his good days?"

She smiled and said to no one in particular, "Oh I think we

may have finally found someone that can handle Old Tom, haven't we? Have a nice morning Rider."

As he walked out the door to load the pickup Rider spoke over his shoulder, "Let's go you contrary old buzzard, we've got fence to build." He didn't look back to see if one or both of them were smiling, but he suspected they both shared a quiet giggle.

They drove up into one of the fields and stopped near a pond that was created thanks to beaver and strolled over to a fence that was lying on the ground. In the fall of each year Tom lays down almost thirty miles of fence and in the spring he rebuilds and puts them back up. Every 50' there is a permanent steel fence post that stays upright year round and in between these posts are cottonwood 'dancers', these being 3" diameter 4' tall poles that the four strands of barbed wire are stapled to. Cutting new dancers and stapling the wire to them every 8' was their project on this morning. Each permanent post also had a dancer that looped a wire over top of that post and that is how the fence was held up.

This was the first section of pasture being 'refenced' this spring and Tom said that he expected the first load of cattle to be delivered any day from the winter range, so he was under a bit of pressure to get this first pasture fenced in preparation for delivery. He wanted the fence up because he didn't want to ride all over hell just to keep a few stragglers in with the group. Rider and Tom worked well together and neither spoke much while setting to work. Rider made sure that he did most of Tom's work without Tom feeling that he wasn't pulling his weight even at his advanced age. Tom was tough of mind and spirit, and equally tough around people, as Rider had learned very quickly. After a solid morning Rider was loading the truck while Tom was leaning against the side while sizing up the beaver dam. "Rider, can you swim?"

"Better than a fish Sir", Rider allowed.

"Ever use dynamite?" Tom asked.

"Never have, but I got a feeling I'm gonna learn tomorrow,"

Rider said with a smile while looking at the beaver dam.

Tom cracked a rare smile and they headed back to see Gladys and assumed lunch would be on the table when they arrived, and it of course was. After lunch Gladys climbed up in the pickup cab with Tom driving and Rider riding shotgun. Tom turned into a completely different person at the farm store in Heber City. He was affable, everyone knew his name and greeted him warmly and loaded the back of his pick up without asking- even the dynamite and caps. Once back in the truck he returned to his normal belligerent, self serving self.

The next morning just after breakfast a Forest Service vehicle pulled into the yard and the Ranger had a conversation with Tom. He motioned for Rider to join them and after introductions the Ranger said that the passes to the north still were impassable due to twenty feet of snow. This meant that Rider wasn't going anywhere anytime soon so he started loading Tom's pickup for the days' work.

Back at the beaver dam Rider eased into the snow supplied chilly water in just his buckskin pants. Once he got his footing Tom handed him three dynamite charges and instructed Rider where to place them. This done, Rider got out of the water and Tom set off the charges a few moments later. It was obvious that Tom knew what he was doing because the force of the simultaneous blasts blew out the dam away from where they were standing. No actual beaver or pieces thereof were to be found, so Rider figured the critters weren't at home at the time of the blast.

The rest of the day they cut more dancers and put up more fence. Rider could see lots of tree carvings high up in the fast growing cottonwood trees. The carvings widened out as the trees grew. Tom said most, if not all of these carvings were his, as he truly enjoyed the craft.

At one point Rider spied a poem etched into the bark that read;

"Out here

lots of cattle,

plenty grass,

and a horses ass"

Tom said they would be on horseback the following morning to work on the fence at the top corner of the first pasture and he should put Jelly in with Tom's horse for the night so they can get acquainted.

Rider was up before Tom the next morning and was already placing the wood stock side rails that fit in Tom's pickup so he could haul stock. He had Jelly saddled and loaded with the help of a ramp shortly after breakfast and Tom went out to saddle his own horse despite Rider's offer to assist. He had a halter on his eighteen year old buckskin gelding and was carrying the headstall in his left hand. His horse followed him out of the corral and Tom just got up in the cab, put the truck in gear and started out of the yard leaving the horse standing in the yard. While the truck was moving forward, Tom's horse simply trotted after it and hopped up in the bed next to Jelly and Tom drove off.

Rider had never seen such a thing but did not want to act too impressed, so he simply rolled down his window and gazed at the scenery for a few moments before saying, "Glad your horse decided to come along, Tom." Tom didn't even bat an eyelash.

Semi trucks loaded with cattle started lining up outside the yard at around 9am the next morning. Both Jelly and Tom's horse were already saddled and Rider was instructed to mount up and lead Tom's horse to the newly fenced pasture about a mile away. Tom would ride in one of the trucks. Rider tied the horses to trees and sat down in the green grass overlooking the reservoir while waiting for the trucks to roll in, ten in all. It was quite a sight to see the semi's turn off the gravel road and directly up into the fields and make sweeping turns so they could back their trailers into the pasture opening. Five hundred cattle were off-loaded that morning and after the trucks left Tom and Rider mounted up and gently pushed the cows to the top edge of the pasture. Seven hundred more cows would arrive during the next days.

The owners of the cattle secured a six thousand acre permit each year to range their cows, and they pay Tom to be their cowboy, as the Forest Service requires. The Rangers monitor the condition of the range and tell Tom when the herd has to be moved so as not to decimate the earth in a particular spot by overgrazing. Mostly the Rangers defer to Tom's judgment as he has been caring for both the cows and the range for half a century, but mostly because Tom's personality keeps them at a distance. The herd is moved every ten days or so and Tom keeps them bunched and moving following the older lead cows who know the drill by heart. Rider stayed on until the second and third pasture fences were completed and then prepared to try the passes, hoping the snow had melted sufficiently to get across and up into Wyoming. The evening before Rider left he thanked Tom and Gladys for the work and generosity, and Tom asked if Rider would stay on til winter, already knowing the answer. This was likely the closest Tom could ever come to saying 'thank you', or expressing appreciation for another's' efforts. He paid off Rider in cash, shook his hand and went to his chair to watch evening TV.

Just for spite and to express his heartfelt thanks quietly to Gladys, Rider helped with the dishes. Gladys smiled.

31.

Sparklers

Three miles north of Strawberry and already up in the hills, Rider turned in his saddle for a final peek at the verdant valley below where he had spent the past two weeks. He turned north from the forest service trail and immediately started climbing into a lush narrow draw. Three hours, two moose and one bear later Rider topped out on a foot deep snow covered 8500' ridge. Since south facing hillsides are generally drier than the north facing brethren, Rider stayed along the southern face of the ridge as much as possible. Not that he had anything to worry about this early in the spring, but just to be safe he didn't want to skyline himself by riding the ridge crest.

Unfortunately the ridge started to angle back to the south so Rider crossed over the top and started again in a northwesterly direction. Few things in life are funnier than watching horses ski down a mountain side with their front legs splayed out while they tuck their butts in and slide along. Once they started losing their grip on the ground Rider simply stepped out of the saddle, let go of the reins and watched them slide down to the treeline 100' below where they regained purchase. They finally stood up and gazed at Rider in a somewhat undignified manner waiting for Rider to stop giggling and stroll down to join them so they all could head off into the woods and out sight of the gods. By late afternoon they had crested the first pass under threatening skies and were fortunate to be heading down the other side as the snow began to fall.

Getting buried by a blinding snowfall can happen quickly that high up and Rider had hustled to get through the first pass unscathed, especially in avalanche country. He made camp with just enough light to do so next to a small stream, fashioned a shelter out of pine boughs, high lined the horses and was immediately asleep.

Waking early due to the cold, Rider saddled in a light snowfall thankful that less than a foot of snow had collected. An early morning 1500' pull in a two mile range was the order of the morning in order to access the 12000' Bald Mountain Pass in the High Uintas mountain range. With a nasty storm threatening from the west Rider did not want to be caught on the wrong side of the five mile long pass and potentially get caught like the Donner Party did more than a century ago. Darkness was beginning to descend just after 2pm as the spring storm was moving in on top of Rider. He began to seek a shelter to get out of the impending weather and spend the long, long night.

Hail intermixed with a driving rain made life difficult as Rider was constructing a tipi shelter under some large pine trees with a small corral sized circle of grass right in front. On the far side of the clearing, maybe 60' away was the shore of a high mountain lake. Rider was able to drag a half dozen downed cottonwood poles to lash to the trees to form enough of a fence that the horses wouldn't bother and wander; he hobbled Chaaco and staked Jelly anyway. He also made enough room for the horses to get under the trees for some shelter. As the dark afternoon wore on the rain and hail turned to a thick wet snow and began collecting on Rider's shelter, which was just fine with him. The snow blanket would make his shelter a little cozier and it was easier to kindle a fire without the rain.

His aromatic, spongy, and freshly cut pine bough bed intermixed with the scents of leather and horse sweat seemed to warm his nest even more. Resting after all the work Rider arranged the firewood he had collected so he could continue to move it along into the fire as the long branches burned without leaving his shelter during the night. The wind wasn't quitting and a cold rain returned as his small fire flickered in the darker than normal evening. He spent the evening searing pieces of sausage on a stick while sitting wrapped in his blanket. Every now and then the camp fire would spark up enough to illuminate the clearing where Jelly was comfortably munching on grass with Chaaco doing the same thing near the lake edge. One of the squalls passed directly through the clearing with the rain falling more horizontal than vertical and the lightning and thunder getting stronger by the second.

An incredible thunderclap accompanied by a lightning bolt striking not more than 30' away exploded Rider to awaken in time to see an illuminated Jelly with all four hooves in the air as if he was levitating and appeared to be momentarily covered with 4th of July sparklers. He heard Chaaco thrashing through the woods and Jelly returned to earth just in time to rare up with such force that the stake pin flew out of the ground and dangled over his butt as he skedaddled into the woods also.

Rider figured the horses wouldn't go too far and would likely find each other in the darkness but he couldn't risk being set afoot, so he decided to go fetch them while they were close. He slipped on his already soaked moccasins and buckskin shirt, leaving his pants nice and dry in his bed, and ventured out into the ice cold driving rain to find his horses.

After thirty minutes he could hear Jelly's stake pin clanging off some rocks and ten minutes later found the horse. He led Jelly back to the clearing with Chaaco hopefully following along. He got the stake pin back in the ground, stripped his wet shirt and moccasins off and dried off as best he could before crawling back into his nest. The storm began to pass out, and so did Rider.

32.

Mosquito Days

Rider lit a cigar amidst the morning drizzle while he and his horses were watching the first of four moose cross his path on this day. Not even the dour weather could spoil his mood as they spent half the day descending out of the snow and back into more reasonable elevations for human habitation. The elevation was still above a mile high but the land began to flatten out a bit, with game trails winding through the hills to follow. The whole day was a gentle ride downhill with short bursts of light rain, and numerous stops to clear away freshly blown down trees from the trails. To Rider's great surprise and delight, a high country lodge serving snowmobilers and hunters came into view just before dusk, and a hot meal and hail squall later he was snuggled into his blankets in a shed next to a small corral where his horses were contently munching on early spring grass.

He learned that Evanston, Wyoming was 30 miles to the north which was the perfect distance to allow Rider to schedule his upcoming days so he could pass around or through the town at night hopefully undetected, as he had with other towns. The Bear River made for a wonderful guide as it ran in the same direction as Rider was heading, so the next few days he would not have to worry about water or grass for his horses, nor fodder for his own self. When camping next to the river, Rider would set out half a dozen gig lines into the water and was usually successful in catching dinner by the time the horses were brushed, settled and hooves checked. He had whittled little sticks down to the size of a large pencil lead, a little more than an inch long. He pointed both ends and fire hardened them and attached them to 3' long cordage he enjoyed making from the inner bark of trees in his spare time. He tied these little sticks in a groove in the middle and baited them with worms or grubs, so that the stick was plastered alongside the cordage. When a fish swallowed the bait, the stick would release and be perpendicular to the line and therefore Rider's dinner. The fish he caught were mostly no more than 10" long; the bigger ones usually broke away. Sometimes he could just stand in the shallows and catch fish in his hands or thrust them onto the bank. He had a small fry pan in his kit and he liked to fillet the fish and cook with whatever berries or leaves he could conjure up.

He made it through Evanston just before dawn with no one the wiser and the valley he entered was between two sets of mountains as it widened out into sagebrush covered hills. The river angled more east than he wanted to go so he hugged the foothills on the western slope. He was still traveling in 6000' terrain and he was thankful that even as the days got longer the nights were cool enough for good sleeping.

On the afternoon of the second day past Evanston, he passed through Woodruff, Utah. Woodruff is one of many outlying small towns in this part of the country that was started by Mormons in the late 1800's to secure their hold on their 'religious' region. These small towns generally had their best days in the early 1900's when small farms were still economically feasible. Now they are either ghost towns or the populations dwindled enough to wish they would be. It was too early to stop and the day was warming up so Rider continued along toward the next town he was told of only a few miles north. His plan was to head into the hills above town, camp and then walk into town in the morning and resupply.

The afternoon got hotter and the 'few miles north', he had been told of in Woodruff by an old lady turned out to be a half day's ride. The 12 miles likely seemed like a 'few miles north' to an old lady in a car, but on horseback at a walk the day became longer than he had hoped. Rider and the horses were caked with sticky dust when they spied Randolph, Utah a mile distant so

Rider started to angle through the sagebrush up into the nearby mountain foothills. Bad idea.

Almost instantly Rider and the horses were swarmed by blankets of mosquitoes so Rider kicked Jelly into a lope to try to get into the trees in hopes the skeeters would lay off once in the woods. It soon became evident that their movement through the sagebrush was spooking up more skeeters than they could possibly outrun and the horses started to crow hop and buck. Rider headed for a copse of trees, swung out of the saddle and stripped the gear off of both horses, tied them and quickly rolled up in his blanket to get out of the bugs. Hot, sweaty, sticky and now rolled up in a thick blanket with the remaining heat of the day still in force, Rider suffered almost to the point of exasperation. After more than an hour rolled up in the blanket furnace the sun slowly went away so did the bugs. It was like a switch was turned off at a certain temperature, for the skeeters disappeared after almost two hours of the onslaught.

Chaaco showed little visible signs of the attack but Jelly was covered with mosquito bump bites from head to toe. Now dark, Rider tacked up and walked the horses to town where he had seen some stockyards when he first saw the town, and led the horses into one of the corrals. He filled a stock tank from a frost-free spigot, and rubbed the horses down for more than an hour. Jellys bumps disappeared after a late night bath applied by Rider and soon after Rider stripped down and laid down in the cool water of the stock tank himself and enjoyed a midnight bath and a cigar. He also emptied the last of his whiskey.

All refreshed in the morning Rider led the horses into and through town. As he tied his horse to a hitch rail outside a historical cabin across from a café, Rider noticed a poster in a shop window inviting one and all to that year's Town of Randolph's annual festival entitled, "Mosquito Days".

He wished he would have known that yesterday.

33.

Little Snakes

The road out of Randolph headed northeast and after restocking his soft panniers, Rider set out in a NNW direction toward Bear Lake, a 20-mile long body of water that is bisected by the Idaho border. Rider was told that the lake was beautiful but the entire area was littered with rattlesnakes. Rider made it to the south end of the lake a couple hours before dark. Even then he could see the aquamarine colored lake, a color of water that looked like it belonged in a tropical setting. He could easily envision why the fur trapping rendezvous were held on this site in 1827 and 1828. He could imagine the valley littered with different tribal tipis, bakers tents offering wares and traders tents throughout the valley.

He walked his horses across the two-lane highway and tied them to a fence next to a small ice cream stand that fortunately was open. While enjoying a chocolate milk shake, burger and fries at a picnic table a police car rolled in. Rider immediately thought of the buffoon of a Sheriff back in Bluff that ordered him out of the State, and thought it ironic that he had only another 10 miles of Utah to deal with and here was the first cop he had seen since then. This Sheriff was a quite friendly chap and introduced himself while asking if Rider needed a place to crash and put up his horses. He pointed out a small house down the street that had a horse trailer parked in the driveway and a fenced backyard that had knee high grass in it. He said Rider was welcome to sleep in the trailer and put his horses in the yard. Just as they were about to engage in a real discussion the Sheriff got a call on the radio so he waved goodbye and was off with his siren blaring.

Rider got to sleep in the trailer out of reach of the rattlesnakes while not worrying about Jelly and Chaaco wandering off during the night. He had a good long sleep without a mosquito in sight. Leaving before the little community of less than 200 souls woke up, Rider walked most of the pleasant day along the dirt road that hugs the eastern shore of the lake. There were isolated cabins along the way, too early in the season to be occupied, but some were. Shortly after crossing into Idaho Rider stopped and chatted with a retired couple from Evanston. They were working in the yard and preparing their cabin for the summer season and enjoyed learning of Rider's journey. The woman disappeared for a few moments as the husband began telling of how a young boy had recently died from snakebites. Seems the boy and his father were fishing along the lake edge and the kid went to dig for worms. He had stuffed the worms he found in his pocket and asked his father if worms bite. Unfortunately the kid had stuffed his pocket with rattlesnake hatchlings instead of worms, and died before the father could get the child to a hospital. The woman reappeared with a sandwich and a coke, but also with swelled eyes indicating that these folks were somehow acquainted with the victim. Seeing this Rider thanked them for their kindness and rode off, not wishing to entertain the gent by listening to the sad tale any further. Reaching the north shore of the lake far sooner than he thought he would, Rider pondered whether to make camp amidst the snakes or move on to the unknown yet again. It was a cool, sunny day with a constant breeze and a large sand bar heading into the lake somehow called to Rider.

He had not seen a human for hours and this part of the lake appeared completely uninhabited, so he stripped off the gear and decided to take the horse for a swim. The horses splashed around in wither height water and Chaaco learned that bucking had no effect on the man on her back, even when he was encouraging her to do so. Rider covered the horses with water he collected in his hat, did his laundry and laid in the sun wearing only a loincloth while the horses stood in knee deep water munching on green grass poking through the surface. An hour later he was back in the saddle and the little crew were all clean and refreshed. A wide lush green valley angled in the direction he was going and lots of sun was left in the day so off he went.

All thoughts of snakes disappeared from his thinking.

34.

Peg Leg

One of the more colorful characters from the fur trapping, mountain man heyday was a legend named Peg Leg Smith. Rider had spent countless hours reading books about this period of North American history and was tickled to be riding through the same country as those hombre's did back in the 1820's. The story goes that Smith got shot in his leg while beaver trapping when he was in his late teens. Left for dead by his companions with winter coming on, Smith managed to survive the winter, but only after cutting off his own gangrenous leg with a butcher knife to survive. Twenty years later found him in possession of a large stock of Andalusian horses he stole from the rich Spanish hacienda's in California, and headed for the area around the town site of Dingle, Idaho, where Rider just happened to be standing at the time. Irrigation projects over the years had drained out the area somewhat, but this valley was still lush. Smith settled into this area and built a trading post on a no longer visible island in the middle of the Bear River. This post became a favorite stop on the Oregon Trail and his name is one of the most popularly referenced characters from the diaries of many who made the trip along the famous trail that passed nearby. Rider would now follow that trail just as the settlers had back then. In many places in the valley the wagon ruts are still visible even more than 150 years later.

Smith's story doesn't end with cutting off his own leg however, as Rider later learned. Seems that after being forced off his post by the Mormon settlers, Peg Leg buried his 'favorite' wife, Mountain Fawn, in the nearby hillside in a standing position so she could see the lake forever. In the same large hole he buried her two favorite horses, food and money so she would not want in her next life. Rider suspected that the ordeal of cutting off one's own leg might have made ol' Pegleg just a bit 'touched', as the Indians would say, so they left him alone.

35.

Old Homes

It was getting to be about time to find a nest for the night and Dingle seemed ghostlike so Rider headed up the valley. The thunderstorms that had been chasing him all day finally caught up to him but not before he had made a shelter in a copse of young cottonwood trees and had a small fire going. He had stripped off the branches from a bunch of the saplings and bent them so as to form a small cabana like structure. Covering this with pine boughs and roofing it with large pieces of pine bark stripped from nearby standing dead trees made for a warm and dry nest. He had time to roll down a large stone and place it opposite the opening of his cabana and laid his fire next to it so the rock acted as a heat reflector. He had a couple flat rocks warming in the fire just in case he wanted to slip them under his pine bough mattress to keep him warm all night, but he didn't think he would need them. The thunderstorm gave way to a steady rain and Rider was content that his horses would not challenge the highline they were tied to about 50 yards away.

In addition to Dingle, the valley was dotted with similar little towns named Paris, Ovid, Wardboro, Bloomington, Bennington and Georgetown; all settled by Mormons as decreed by the powers that were from the head honcho back in the tabernacle. All had seen better days and many have since been purchased or swallowed by large ranches. Mormons, historically known to be given to a healthy appreciation of history have maintained many of the original settler's dwellings and town buildings to this day. Rider enjoyed passing these places during his long ride on the next day that ended at Soda Springs, Idaho.

36.

Golden Tara

Rider's plan was to find some stockyards or the site of the County Fairgrounds as is often found in the largest town in any county in the west, and Soda Springs seemed to fit the bill. He rode in to the outskirts of the town at around 6pm and immediately spied a motel with a public phone booth, so he dismounted to check the phonebook for the address of the fairgrounds. Before he could open the book he was startled by a soft squeaky voice asking, "Are you a real mountain man?"

Peeking out from the other side of Jelly's right foreleg was a little blonde haired girl that was cuter than a bug. The girl had now wrapped herself around Jelly's leg and was smiling up at Rider who was now at a loss for words. Her grandma was emerging from the motel office with a big smile and said, "Tara, did you ask the nice man if you could touch his horse?"

"Well she seems to be glued on so even if Jelly, that's my horse's name, wanted to shuck her off I doubt he'd be able to," Rider smiled as he gently rubbed Jelly's nose. Grandma gently peeled the little girl off the horse and out of flying hoof distance just in case and asked if she could help.

"Could you direct me to the fairgrounds or a stockyard where I can put up my horses for a couple days; they need a break and I'm kinda wantin' to rest a spell myself", said Rider.

Before Grandma could pipe up the little girl commanded, "Stay here!"

"Thank you young lady, but I need a place to put up my horses"

"You can keep them at my Grandpa's house", little Tara said. Grandma, a part Ute Indian named Delores John, smiled at the persistence of her granddaughter, as did Rider. "Tara, you run in and call Grandpa to see if it's alright," and the girl tore off for the motel office.

After Rider introduced himself Delores said that she was sure it would be fine and Grandpa's home was only a ½ mile away, so he could check-in and unload his gear into his newly rented motel room.

"Let's start with three days if that is okay?" asked Rider, and Delores said that would be fine.

Tara said that grandpa was expecting them and Rider said, "Okay young lady you got yourself a deal but on one condition; you have to ride one of the horses over to his house, deal?"

"I like the black one."

"Her name is Chaaco and she was raised by a Navaho girl about your age way down in Utah, so she'll like you", Rider said as he lifted the little girl aboard.

Ten minutes later Rider was shaking hands with Bob and Carolyn Rigby, plus others floating about. The Rigby's were grandparents through and through, the exact definition of unconditional love and warmth for all their grandchildren. Whether they were products of one night stands or broken marriages, they didn't care, and made sure the children thought none of it either.

Bob was a gent of stocky build, a couple inches shorter than Rider's six foot height, with slicked back salt n' pepper hair and ever present sunglasses. He led Rider, with Tara still glued to Chaaco's back, out behind their ranch style house in a small neighborhood that bordered the wilderness, to a fenced in yard that hadn't been mowed yet this spring. Rider walked the perimeter while Bob leaned on the fence and then unclipped the halter ropes and looped them over the fence.

"I imagine Grandpa will need these halters until Tara's bedtime", Rider mused.

Bob just shook his head and asked if Rider was hungry.

"Bob, I'm always hungry and I thank you for the offer, but right now my plan is to take my first bath in two months and collapse in a real bed since then also, til whenever."

124

"I certainly understand that. Let me run you back to the hotel and I'll check in on you tomorrow afternoon sometime; sound alright?" Bob offered.

"Sounds wonderful and we'll square up for the pasture when I regain consciousness, okay?"

Bob slapped Rider on the shoulder blade and said, "Sounds right fine by me young man!"

Rider was sitting in a chair outside his motel room when Bob pulled in at 2pm.

"Up for a ride" asked Bob.

"Absolutely Sir", answered Rider, who had shaved his entire head and felt 20 pounds lighter after laying in the bathtub for a couple hours and shedding three months of trail dust.

Bob took Rider on a tour of the historical sites around his hometown and there were plenty. Soda Springs was a renowned area during the fur trapping days in the early 1800's and Oregon Trail travelers in the 1850's. After negotiating the South Pass to the east, Soda Springs was a welcome sight for good grass and water was always present. The area is littered with natural carbonated water springs that are especially wonderful for bathing. Bob's home is on the site of a fort called Camp Conner that was built by Mormon's and active in the mid 1860's before being purposefully razed so the Indians couldn't use it. As Bob drove around he narrated about how some wagon trains camped here or there, and who they were led by. This information is still being carried by those given to honoring the history of the town even though the events took place almost 150 years ago. After a few hours of driving they ended up at Bob's house where quite a gaggle of people milled about. Word of Rider's arrival had turned Bob's house into a neighborhood cookout complete with local politicos and such. Eventually Rider made his way to a picnic table in the back yard where he could see every kid in Idaho leaning on the fence asking Tara questions about the horse, Chaaco which she was glued to. Carolyn said that Tara was up before breakfast and had been sitting on Chaaco for the better part of the whole day. The cookout was still going strong at dusk when Rider slipped back to the motel for another dose of endless sleep.

The only achievement for Rider the next day was to gaze at a map in the motel office and try to figure out how he was going to cross the Snake River and get his ass home.

37.

Oregon Trail

As with most of the 'trails' Rider had followed or crossed since Cloverdale, the Oregon Trail that he now found himself on followed the natural flow of geography. And additionally, most of the 'trails' were now roads or highways with cities, towns and neighborhoods on either side; all of which Rider wanted to avoid travelling near.

He was facing about a three day ride to get to the Snake River and limited methods of crossing it unless he wanted to get wet. The river is much wider than it was 150 years ago thanks to dams and other human intervention, so rather than seek out a suitable spot to cross, Rider simply opted for the nearest bridge and headed towards Blackfoot, Idaho.

The first day out of Soda Springs was a long and pleasant day that ended up in the ghost town of Chesterfield, Idaho. Many buildings still stand and some are being restored by descendants of the Mormons that built the town in the late 1800's. The town site was very similar to that of Strawberry with plenty of grass, easily accessed water and hillside building sites to keep out of the spring floods. There were remnants of a corral and a shed so Rider had a restful sleep not having to worry about his horses on a stake or in hobbles.

It was always a bonus to have an enclosure for his horses.

The next two days were mile eaters but without worry. It was hot but the terrain was dotted by alders, cottonwoods and pine trees all whispering their own melodies in the breeze. It got so that Rider began to be able to define which trees were around by both their scents and songs, given the different shapes and foliage singing in the wind. It reminded him of the brilliance of harbor bells tolling at different pitches so seafarers could figure out which harbor they were near when in thick fog.

Along about mid afternoon three days out of Soda Springs, Rider passed by the remnants of one of the Fort Hall's, meaning that the Fort had been relocated three times back in the day.

He was still on the Shoshone/Bannock reservation but had not seen any evidence of it like the reservations to the south. He stopped at the first ranch he came to outside of Blackfoot because he could see that getting through town on horseback was not a smart move. The entire town was between him and not only the Snake River, but also a major highway complete with interchanges. He would have to load the horses on a trailer and have them driven across. He hated doing this because it meant sicophanting himself to the modern world, but the realities were the realities; it wasn't 1840 anymore. Just as he dismounted to open the ranch gate a pickup truck towing an 8-horse gooseneck trailer slowed down and looked him over. A young gent in his thirties named Gary leaned out of his window and said with a big grin, "Where the hell did you come from?"

"Not sure you'd believe me if I told ya", Rider said matching smiles.

"Looks like you come a long ways wherever it was."

"I started down in Old Mexico back in March and I'm headed for home on the Snake over in Washington. Might I be able to hire your outfit to get me across that mess of highway I'm lookin' at?"

"Let me turn around and we'll run 'em in."

"Jeez you are a freakin' saint. If you were younger, better lookin' and female I'd try to hug ya" Rider said.

Gary pushed his sweat stained straw hat back on his head and drove down the dirt road, swung the rig around and pulled up ahead of Rider, who was loosening the cinches on both horses. Gary swung the door open and Rider looped the reins around the saddle horns, slapped Jelly on the butt and both horses hopped in without a word otherwise as Gary shut the door.

They unloaded the horses at Rockford, Idaho after a 30 minute drive through Blackfoot and across the bridge that got Rider on the north side of the Snake. His home near the ghost town of Almota, Washington was on the north side of the Snake also, so he felt a measure of accomplishment in knowing that he might not have to deal with that river again. Rockford was small enough to be a ghost town with a farm store, a factory and a few streets being the only signs of life. Gary wouldn't take any money for the ride but asked if Rider would send him a book if he ever wrote one about his journey. They departed pals and Rider made camp just west of town in a small copse of trees.

Byway Rt. 39 was running west and the terrain dictated that Rider do also. If it was good enough for the folks that used the Oregon Trail back then, it was likely a good move for Rider now. He knew that he wanted to angle in more of a northwest direction but the dry lava beds of the Snake River Plains in July made that choice more foolish than less. He would have liked to hug closer to the Snake River but civilization was in the way. The plains he was on made for easy travel with the road always in sight for there really was nowhere else to go.

It was mid July and the days were hot. The exposed lava was too hot to touch but it could be mostly avoided. Once away from the small towns Rider could cut cross country only to be turned back south toward the road because the entire terrain was planted with potatoes, beets and grains. He rode past the American Falls Reservoir, created by a dam of the same name and was able to skulk through Aberdeen, Idaho in the middle of the night with nary a human about. He camped for two days on the westernmost point of the reservoir and was able to cut cross country again, or so he was told, toward Lake Walcott and the little community of Minidoka, Idaho, where he could resupply. All along the route there were little 'ranchettes' where he could water his horses and refill his canteen without anyone being the wiser, for most had small corrals for their personal horses and whatnot, and Rider was traveling at night. He figured it was a three day ride to the Minidoka through the dusty sagebrush of the high plains but after three months of desert, the plains worried him little. Throughout the trip he tried to keep to a routine of 20 miles the first day, 15 the next and 10 miles on the third day followed by a day of rest. The terrain and civilization dictated the course of travel, but he wanted to preserve his horses nonetheless.

At Minidoka he was a day's ride away from the Oregon Trail with a clear understanding as to why few ventured off of it to the north as he had. The ground was getting increasingly tough with decaying lava rocks dotting the surface in between expansive, dull green sagebrush plants. Dried up thistle tumbleweeds adhered to sagebrush clumps until the next stiff breeze came along, and Rider hadn't felt one in a couple days. Thankfully the nights were still cool.

There was an abandoned ranch house just outside of Minidoka, for there wasn't really a town per say, but it did have a small grocery store where Rider was able to resupply and get information about his intended direction. He could see mountains far off to the north but suspected the terrain held no byways or roads for a reason. He still needed to be more than a couple hundred miles west of where he was so the question in his mind was whether to make that jump now or later. The terrain, barbed wire fences, a railroad track and a byway heading west made the decision for him, so he continued west keeping highway 24 always in sight.

He camped on the north side of Dietrich, Idaho late afternoon on the third day out of Minidoka near an airplane landing strip in a copse of trees. He had deposited his horses in a small abandoned corral complete with stock tank and a frost free water hydrant. He tacked a note on a wooden post next to the hydrant explaining who the horses were and where he could be found, about a ½ mile away. Small towns with about a couple hundred people are always mindful of any changes in their landscape so Rider wanted to be as invisible as possible for the two days he planned on resting out of site. By the time anyone got around to seriously asking about the two strange horses in the old corral, he planned to be gone. Fortunately he was able to travel far enough away from the road so that the occasional pickup truck wouldn't see him and his string. He had breakfast at the only establishment in town and resupplied there also. He was hoping the old gal at the counter wouldn't ask too many questions and she didn't, thankfully. It was quite clear that she was much keener on girls than she was on boys.

On the morning of the third day he was off, heading straight towards the mountains that were becoming more distinct with each step. He was anxious to be back in the cooler mountains and away from people. He employed an old cavalry trick to speed up the walk of his horses by swinging his feet in the stirrups to and fro so the horses would match his pace; and they did.

38.

Sawtooths

The landscape was just desolate, without character. He was told that a long day in the saddle heading northwest would bring him to the Big Wood River, which he would follow past a large reservoir and then it would turn directly west. Somewhere along this stream he would cut north into the naked foothills of the Sawtooth Range. He came upon the river sooner than expected and it turned north just like it was supposed to. Traveling near rivers was always wonderful because there was usually cover to be found, available water and generally trails along the banks. It was late July and the lava fields were convection oven hot but not so much that the heat forced Rider to travel at night. He started at first light and rode until the sun forced siesta time, and it was a pleasant way to travel.

Two days past Dietrich found him along the road that paralleled the western shore of the Magic Reservoir. He could see a lakeside community in the distance but he decided to bypass it and keep going. His horses were well fed and watered and his larder was stocked with granola bars, a stick of cheese, a roll of summer sausage and some crackers. He was anxious to climb again into the mountains, and they were getting closer and closer. He stayed along the Camas Creek bed heading directly west and made camp.

He crossed Highway 20 first thing and walked along a byway that paralleled it all the way to Fairfield, Idaho, where he put up the horses at the fairgrounds and took a motel room for a couple days. He wanted a good rest for both himself and his horses before tackling the mountains. It was here that he realized just how close he was to finishing his journey. It was near August and he figured it would take him a month of comfortable travel to get across the Camas Prarie and through the Sawtooth and River of No Return Mountains. Once through the mountains he would head toward Elk City, Idaho, and after two weeks of travel along side roads he had traveled by car in the past, he'd be home. That would put him home about mid September, unless he lollygagged too much in the mountains.

He was saddling his mounts just before dawn on the third day in Fairfield and looking forward to moving again. Other than pleasantries to waitresses and motel clerks, Rider hadn't said a word to a soul it seemed like for weeks. Now he was about to embark on a journey into some of the most remote mountains in the lower 48, and it was more likely than not that he wouldn't be seeing another human to speak to for a month.

Out of the prairie and into bald rolling foothills, Rider was indiscernibly climbing. As the trees became more prevalent so did the available water, with little creeks and streams throughout the countryside. By the end of the day Rider was on a dirt road with a forest service sign on it that signaled the beginning of their jurisdiction. To Rider, that meant clean, crisp high mountain air was soon to be had. He hadn't seen a vehicle all day and was thankful for it. The following morning he crossed the south fork of the Boise River and left the road on a game trail headed straight north, and up.

For the next week he wandered in amongst a series of high aquamarine mountain lakes that he could almost see the bottom from his perch on the ridges above. When the time was right, he simply chose a lake to camp by and fish for dinner. Back in Fairfield he had bought packets of powdered butter, and frying fish with that powder would be a real treat. Traveling through the Sawtooths was proving to be a breeze as the pine tree laden lush green valleys all seemed to interconnect without too much geographical obstructions. He wasn't using up his supplies as he thought he might for water was as abundant as the fish he caught. The craggy edges of the peaks above were far more abrupt than he had thought they would be, and the given name for the mountain range was apt; that being an upturned crosscut logging saw with the saw teeth resembling the Sawtooths. It was on the tenth day out of Fairfield that Rider exited the Sawtooth country and crossed Rt. 21 and entered the Frank Church River of No Return Wilderness Area. The mountain travel had been days of bear, moose, mountain goat, deer and elk encounters, all of which belonged there just as much as Rider did. He was truly part of the natural flow of nature.

39.

Lazy Days

A Forest Service road headed west as did the valley, so Rider did also. He stayed along this dirt road for two days and then the road turned directly north as the bald eagle flies, and there were plenty to be seen. He was passed by one pickup truck hauling a camper, and both horses simply stopped and watched the rattling contraption speed by, leaving them in a cloud of dust. City folk are simply ignorant when around stock out in the country, they don't know or care about slowing down around critters. This Forest Service road was married to what Rider thought was the Payette River, but there was no one to talk to in order to confirm it for the six days he was on it. He wasn't eating up miles but he didn't much care. The fishing was good and his supply of crackers, sausage and cheese was also. The water from the river was cool and refreshing, and he didn't bother to treat it with iodine to ensure its potability. Most days he would leave the road, cross the creek and camp out of sight. A few dull green small Forest Service pickups passed his camps but he thought it just as well to stay undetected for as long as possible. They might hit him up for a permit or some such thing.

Yellow Pine, Idaho was an unexpected mirage in the middle of the road. Rider had no idea such a place existed, but was absolutely tickled that it did. There was a café, saloon and a motel of sorts. The town had a population of zero, so he was told, but there were plenty of people there anyway to serve hunters, ATV'ers, and snowmobilers in winter. He bought a bag of oats for the horses and penned them just outside of town. Rider spent a couple days eating burgers instead of fish while doting on his horses each day. He could have spent his days making new pals but he was far more comfortable brushing his horses. There was intrinsic comfort in isolation for him after months alone on the trail. After a couple days of beer and burgers he rode west until he latched on to the Salmon River and intended to follow it until Dixie, Idaho, through the Gospel Hump Wilderness.

Riding along the Salmon River was more of the same, easy going life in the mountains, only this time there was a maze of trails that had been cleared by hunting outfitters that had been used for years. It was too early for the outfitters to maintain their trails so Rider was off his horse a dozen times a day to clear off blow downs and deadfalls. He was riding Jelly almost exclusively these days and at times simply let Chaaco follow along unattached. Jelly was 'bomb-proof' by this point, meaning that he would stand still when spooked or something was amiss, and that he followed Rider's rein and leg cues to the letter. The horse was an absolute joy to ride. Chaaco was well trained by this time also, but she had a tendency to avert her attention to places other than Rider's cues at the most inopportune moments. When geography got in the way of riverside travel, there was always a trail into the woods leading up and over it. It was on one of these trails that Rider spied a beautiful bay gelding storming down a nearby ridge. His coat was shiny and the horse was full of piss and vinegar. Once the horse caught wind of Rider's mounts he stopped, stared and aggressively snorted. Chaaco let out a little whinny while Jelly just stood with his head cocked to the right and his ears pricked forward. After a few minutes the horse simply ambled over the rise and Rider turned his mount and continued on. He figured that the horse had been on its own for quite some time, escaped from an outfitter likely, and proving once again that horses take care of themselves much better than humans can.

He rode into the old mining town of Dixie on the last day of August, half wondering if he should just turn around and head back into the mountains. At a hunting lodge he opted for a cup of hot chocolate, since he had never drank a cup of coffee in his life. There were a few groups of campers milling about in preparations for their 'backcountry' horseback adventure, for the lodge was an outfitter also. With all this activity, Rider was able to hide in plain sight by sitting atop a picnic table under a large pine tree while watching the humans and their dynamics. He sat there watching as huge canvas tents, complete with pack stoves and chairs were being lashed to the sides of the pack animals. With the bounty that nature provided, he was somewhat miffed at the amount of groceries these folks stuffed into the large panniers.

He then looked at his small soft panniers and his saddlebags and wondered whether he should have started his journey with a pack animal also. He concluded that simple is better, albeit more risky, but knowing what he now knew about cross country travel, he'd advise anyone else to stick to one animal if at all possible. Once on the trail, a fellow did not need very much.

He hung around for about an hour or so, then moseyed over to his horses and walked them back into the woods until they were out of sight, and again headed north alongside a creek and the dirt road. The creek petered out after a few miles so he made his way across it to make camp, while he still had the water nearby.

Within an hour the next morning the gravel road turned to pavement and he reflected about this with some sadness. He knew the road headed to Elk City, Idaho and he had visited that burg a couple years previous. Elk City was a 4 hour drive from his home, or about a ten day ride on a horse, given the terrain.

From the paved road where he now stood, he knew that his days of back country travel were over, and the road to Lewiston, Idaho was dotted with private homes and barbed wire. At some point he would simply hire a truck and trailer to get him through Lewiston, across the Snake and Clearwater Rivers and drop him off on the river road that led to his home high above the river.

40.

Road Weary

When he struck the Red River that afternoon he decided to make camp and make another ¾ day on the 'morrow. He knew that Elk City was about a mile from the road he was on, and he suspected that he would bypass it and join the south fork of the Clearwater River shortly after the cut-off to the town. Elk City was the site of a minor gold rush in the early 1860's and sustained itself as a town during those early years. The following decade saw an influx of Chinese hoping to tap the gold reserves in some semblance of peace but as with other areas in that time, the white folk about refused to allow those folks from the orient any peace. In other areas in the region the remnants of the presence of Chinese is witnessed by almost inaccessible rock gardens and barricades built on the steep hills above waterways to protect themselves from indiscriminant bullets and rapes. He was a couple miles west of Elk City when he crossed the creek and made camp under some tall pines. The September nights were cool and beginning to evolve into 'crisp' which was just fine with Rider. Now that the road, Rt. 14, had turned west it became a hilly corkscrew but never left sight of the river. He was riding in a canyon and was heading west, albeit slowly because the road continually doubled back on itself in order to follow the terrain. It took him three days to reach the cut-off to Mt. Idaho, which he could see in the distance. He hardly rode his horses on these days, as the roadway was narrow and passing vehicles were generally cruising faster than they should have been. It was safer for his horses and for him to have all feet in the string connected to the ground. His moccasins were holding up pretty well even though the sandy road bed was wearing away the buffalo hide faster than Rider liked. By the time he came upon the cut-off he had had his fill of walking alongside the roadway. The dirt cut-off angled northwest gradually up the hillside in sight of Rt. 14 for quite a distance, and it was a slow and steady pull now that Rider had mounted up on Chaaco.

When he lost site of the paved road below, he left the cut-off road on a game trail directly west and over the steep hill only to rejoin the cut-off on the downward side, saving himself a couple hours of needless riding. Once over the hill he was into suburbia, country style, with private homes every few hundred yards on both sides of the sandy road as he descended back into the Nez Perce section of the Camas Prairie.

The hills in this part of the country are not as abrupt as mountains per say, but are nonetheless formidable enough to define travel routes through them. It seemed like every valley had a road of some kind, whether the destination be a town, (or ghost town), or a private ranch. Unlike forested mountains, a man on horseback could scale any of the hills at any time if he so chose, so getting from point A to point B really was a matter of how hard he wanted to work his mount. With almost 2000 miles on his back trail, and more importantly on his horses back trail, he opted for the least amount of exertion for the horses as possible. That now meant road travel for the most part, as the most direct route to his home was no longer covered with plants and trees, but by asphalt.

41.

Mount Idaho

Rider had just passed through one of the more fabled ghost towns in the inland northwest. For its first twenty years of existence, Mount Idaho was the focal point for the gold mining region, complete with all of the trappings one might find in a mining camp of the time, sans prostitution. Two enterprising gents had carved out a wagon road that reached Lewiston, Idaho from the Elk City region that saved countless miles and reduced burden on the stock that pulled the ore laden wagons. For the privilege of using this road, the gents charged a toll, which most folks gladly paid. After a couple years of successful operation and growth of the town, one of the gents had to sell out because he decided to get in a fight with a cougar, disabling the poor gent forever. Over the next decade or so the town flourished with a bona fide hotel, a stage route and the first white female appeared at some point. How many followed one could only guess but the lore is that women never had to pay to use the toll road, perhaps as an inducement for others to consider setting down roots in Mt. Idaho.

All was fine until the Nez Perce war broke out in the mid 1870's, rendering the supply route to and from Lewiston too risky to venture. When the real killing began in 1877 the large hotel in town was transformed into a triage post and hospital, and some of the casualties were buried nearby with the headstones enduring. Over the next 40 years the town remained stable until a better, albeit longer road was constructed between Elk City and Lewiston, and the town succumbed when the post office finally closed.

42.

Familiar Territory

Once on the valley floor Rider started scouting for water for the horses and a place to pull off to bed down. As always, he wanted to get through town as undetected as possible, but the timing was all wrong to get through Grangeville, Idaho. He needed to rest the horses and still had at least an hour of riding to get to the outskirts of the town, as this he had estimated coming down from Mt. Idaho, where he could see the lay of the land. He wanted to get through the town before dawn, and Grangeville had more sprawl than a town of its size had a right to, but it did. The town was also known as being ultra conservative, with many of its residents being employed by the government and thereby of the officious type, and might not take too kindly to something as out of the ordinary as a gent in buckskins strolling through their little town leading a couple horses. So Rider slowed his pace and finally found a hydrant with a stock tank under it at a workshop just off the road. He lifted the hydrant arm up and let the water flow as each horse greedily dipped their noses into the cool water. Rider walked around the facility but found no one so after the horses drank their fill, he high lined them between some trees far enough off of the two lane road so as not to be seen. He bedded down and drank his fill himself, hoping his pee alarm clock would wake him early enough to get beyond Grangeville before first light.

The pee alarm again worked well. It was still dark and Rider estimated they were walking through the center of Grangeville at about 4am. By 7am he was far enough away from town so that he wasn't passing a driveway every 100 yards or so. He had 14 miles of travel along Rt. 95 which was not overly pleasant, but all the fields were secured with barbed wire so there wasn't much choice. Along the route he had an idea that brightened his day immeasurably. He had been wondering about getting through the sprawling Lewiston area and whether he should just conclude his journey there by hiring a trailer to take him through that town and the 30 miles left to get him to Almota, Wa., and his home.

The road to Lewiston that he was on would mean his travel would be restricted by barbed wire for the 60 miles to Lewiston, and that would be both boring and less than safe. He then remembered that he could eliminate that decision altogether by angling northwest toward the town of Waha, Idaho, and get off the road to boot. He had been to Waha before and the terrain was hilly but the real problem would be figuring out the maze of gravel roads up in those hills. It would be slow going but much more pleasant than strolling along the highway. He would have to find a place to camp to the south of Cottonwood and scoot through just as he did in Grangeville, but Cottonwood was much smaller and he was confident that his pee alarm would wake him in plenty of time to complete the task.

He made it through Cottonwood and tied his horses in a copse of trees and walked back into town in search of a Forest Service or similar road map for the Waha area and to top off his soft panniers. Rider was the first customer of the day at the local grocery store and purchased a map and more apples than usual. He was thankful that he found the map in the store and didn't have to spend half the day in search of one.

Both of his horses thought apples to be better than sugar, but Rider got a box of cubes for them also. The roads leading to Waha were all dirt and gravel in addition to being very hilly. It was only 70 miles to the Lewiston/Clarkston area as the crow flies and if it were a straight line that would be a four day ride. Given the terrain, the winding roads, and allowing for getting lost, Rider hoped to be stuck in the Waha hills for no more than a week. But this was terrain he was used to and very similar to his home on the Snake River. It was mid September and he wasn't concerned about finding water because the brown, dry grass hills always had springs dotting the hills. These were easily spotted by the lush green vegetation that belied their location. Sometimes it took considerable effort to actually get to water as one usually had to cut away the overgrown pricker bushes and perhaps spook out a couple lounging coyotes first. The rattlesnakes usually slithered away without so much as a buzz.

Rider felt kind of like he was cheating by using a map. He also felt it kind of ironic that the first time he used a map on this journey, was for the only region on the trip that he had previously been on. He also knew that if he did not use the map he might get completely turned around and travel useless miles on the wrong roads. The maps also allowed him to cut country directly up and over the rolling hills rather than sticking to the winding roads that simply followed what the terrain allowed. The climbing an average 1000' hill was typically accomplished in eight spurts of stopping and resting the horses so they could catch their breath. Three or four of these pulls a day is about all his horses would be able to muster if he wanted to use them the following day, given their condition after almost 2000 miles of use in six months. With the map in hand, Rider could choose when to leave the road and cut in a more direct line until he ran across the next road, and this he did. A couple miles before reaching the summit of Cottonwood Butte, Rider cut off the road directly west. Rain had started to fall so Rider made a camp and shelter in the trees. There was plenty of grass and Rider set his hat out in the rain to act as a watering trough for the horses. He staked both animals where they could reach the hat but not get their lines tangled. He dug a hole for the hat to sit in so they couldn't tip it over. Rider knew they wouldn't leave the hat even if they broke free. It was only early afternoon but they had awakened early two days in a row so this would be a welcome long day and night of rest. The rain looked like it was going to stick around for more than a day, so Rider settled in with a good book and some cheese. The next morning both horses were looking at Rider with their ears pricked forward, as if to say,

"Let's get going sleepyhead!" The map said that it was about 15 miles as the crow flies to Soldiers Meadow Reservoir, but it was more like twice that along the maze of roads, assuming that he would be able to keep to the ones he was supposed to. Road signs in this part of the country had a habit of disappearing or getting twisted by a passing combine during harvest. He was out of farming country but was close enough to it that the reasoning still applied. He would have liked to make it to the reservoir but it wouldn't bother him if he didn't. The reservoir just made it easier to find a campsite and a shelter-usually under a picnic table in rainy weather, and it still was.

Rider woke unexpectedly well before dawn the next morning and decided to hit the trail while enjoying the earth waking up. They pulled up at the reservoir after only a couple hours and the sun appeared as they approached the water. It was early enough in the day and it was a crisp September day, so Rider chose to head to Lake Waha 10 miles to the northwest and rest for a day or two. There were two choices of roads which led to the lake, either the valley or the ridge, with the ridge being twice as long due to the switchbacks. If Rider was out on a weekend horse ride, he would have opted for the ridge route, but at the end of such a journey as this, he opted for the valley. Either way it was a pleasant day made more appealing by knowing he would end up on the shores of a beautiful lake where he had camped at a few times in years past. It was easy to marvel at Lake Waha just by looking at the terrain surrounding it, and understanding what it was before some ingenious gents dammed up and collected the water that was now in the lake. The land was once arid, rocky and covered with scrub plants. These reservoir projects allowed farmers to irrigate and produce, while also giving life to the south end of Lewiston, called Lewiston Orchards. Someone had to have had great vision to look at scrub land and see the potential.

Rider spent two days on the shore of the lake and would travel at night from this point on until he got across the Snake River for the last time. It was about 20 miles to Hells Gate State Park on the south end of Lewiston and from there he could cross the bridge into Clarkston, Washington, and skirt around the south end of that town and finally cross the Snake again onto Wawawai Canyon Rd. Once on Wawawai Rd, he would have a two day ride to his gate.

It took an hour to drop down out of the hills from the lake after the moon turned on the lights. He had lounged around the lake for two days and was now eager to get home. Once on the flat, the gravel roads stretched out in long, straight paths amidst wheat fields covered with stubble, after being recently harvested. The pungent sweet smell of recently cut plants that had been covered with rain only a few days previous pervaded Rider's senses, as they plodded on.

Homes, if there were any, were set back well off the road, green trees belying their location. At most every crossroad Rider turned left, or west, as he stair-stepped his way closer to the Snake River and the Hells Gate State Park and Campground. Even though Rider had been on these roads before, he was glad that he had the road map and that the road signs were mostly still standing, albeit a few with the obligatory buckshot holes. He rode into Hells Gate just as Lewiston was waking up and took the horses to the swimming area for a quick drink, and then into the farthest campground to remove the saddles and gear. He let the horses graze on the lawn and wondered when they had last done that; eating grass from a 'lawn'. A Park Ranger stopped by and suggested a better site for Rider to spend the day would be on the north side of the park away from people, after Rider told him that he was passing through. He saddled up and led the horses to some trees along a dirt trail where the park was undeveloped and hobbled Jelly. The horses spent the day grazing and drinking out of the Snake and Rider made himself a bed on the round river

143

rocks on the Snake's bank. Before catching a snooze Rider walked back into the park and kicked away a couple of horse dung piles so visitors wouldn't have to step in them, as he told the Ranger he would.

There were just a few RV's in the campground and a retired couple from Utah was sitting outside of one and watching Rider deal with the dung. As he walked by he asked the folks what day it was and they said it was Wednesday. Rider thanked them and kept walking, not wanting to get into a conversation. He was happy to learn that he had arrived in town mid week, thinking that the roads and bridges he would have to cross that evening might not as populated as they might be on a Friday or Saturday. In all he had only about 10 miles and two bridges to negotiate and he would start out at about 10pm. Until then he would spend the day on the river's edge, tossing little sticks upstream, and trying to plunk them with little pebbles as they floated by.

There was more than enough ambient light from the city to saddle up and lead the horses out. He led Jelly for that horse would not spook at anything, even jake brakes from a passing semi truck should that happen. The risk in crossing a bridge is that if the horses get spooked, there is no place to go other than into traffic. He hoped that some fool wouldn't beep their horn also, and by 3am the jaunt was completed, and thankfully no horns were tooted, or air brakes engaged.

He decided to keep going, knowing that the more miles he ate today, the odds of getting home tomorrow got better, and he decided that tomorrow would be the day journey from old Mexico would end.

43.

Final Push

Rider slept off to the side of first parking area along Wawawai Canyon Rd. just past the Steptoe Canyon Rd intersection. He staked his horses on the other side of the road where there was enough green grass to fill the horse's bellies and where a pond was formed by the road berm. If he got an early start he would make it to the submerged ghost town of Wawawai by mid afternoon and he did. The day was cool for mid September and it was a leisurely ride all day.

Wawawai, pronounced like Hawaii, was a thriving orchard town in the late 1800's and early 1900's and produced apples, pears, prunes among other fruits. In the 1960's all the residents knew that they had to leave because a dam was going to be constructed that would give Idaho a seaport and their town would eventually be about 80' under water. In 1975 Lower Granite Dam began to hold back the Snake River that created the lake that exists now, and covers the waterlogged town. Barges bring goods from the coast upriver while hauling wheat and logs from Idaho downriver.

Upon arriving at Wawawai he rested at the boat ramp area and wondered if the afternoon cargo train had passed toward Lewiston yet. He had to skirt around the county park and stroll along the railroad tracks for four miles until he reached his home, and there were a couple of sections that were just barely wide enough to get his horses off the tracks in case the train happened by. He wasn't worried about Jelly, for he had grown up watching the train make its daily to and from run all his life.

Chaaco had only one experience with trains, and remembering the jumping off the tracks back in Utah might come back to haunt her if the train rolled by so close. He decided to chance it, for he would be able to sleep in his own bed for the first time in more than six months, and reintroduce himself to his pups and other horses, and that was inducement enough. The last four miles seemed to take a lifetime and Rider was curious as to how he would feel once he first caught a glimpse of his home. He had thought of and anticipated how he would feel and now was curious to see if any of his internal predictions would come true. Regardless, he knew that this was to be a day, and a feeling, that he would never forget.

Catching sight of Lower Granite Dam from the upriver side caused him a short breathe or two but as his home slowly came into view he surprisingly felt little other than acknowledgement of its' location. He simply knew that this is where he belonged and was gratified to be back. He wound his way to his gate and unlatched it from astride Jelly. Rider had designed this gate a few years prior so that it would automatically swing open, and could be opened from atop a horse. Rider smiled lightly as Jelly remembered that once the gate was unlatched, the horse had to step aside to let it swing open. He knew then that Jelly recognized that he was home and that was the happiest emotion of the day. Once inside the gate he coaxed Chaaco to come along side so he could hold her a little closer as they climbed the steep trail up to the barn and his ranch house. Usually the trail is a one-stop climb but on this day, Jelly was stepping brightly with his head typically cocked to the left and his ears pricked forward. The horse never stopped until he was in the round pen waiting for his saddle to be removed. He also kept his eyes or ears focused on the craggy ridge above that separated the house, corrals and outbuildings from the acres of pasture above, hoping his long lost pals and family would soon appear. Rider had the saddles off and hung in the barn just as the three boxer dogs and the small herd of a dozen horses could be seen cascading over the nearby undulating hills racing toward the corral. Jelly let out a screaming whinny as the stallion led the charge to see his son for the first time in over six months. Chief, Squally John and Gus were yelping uncontrollably as Rider sat on the steps awaiting their arrival to enjoy a reunion sure to be full of boxer slobber. Chaaco was frightened to death to be surrounded by the milling herd of excited horses outside the corral while Jelly was prancing along the inside of the round pen huggin' n' kissin' his old pals. Squally John, the only female amongst the pups couldn't stop peeing she was so happy to be hugged again by Rider. Gus, the youngest, kept his distance a bit but couldn't stay out of Riders' embraces for long. Gus always wanted his lovin' in short spurts. Chief, the eldest and smallest, was typically subdued and quite content to sit next to Rider with one paw in his lap while Rider scratched him behind the ears. It was getting close to dark and Rider wanted to get the horses out into the open range while Chaaco would have plenty of light to explore her new surroundings while fighting off her new family's attentions and affections. He peeled off the dogs and grabbed a bale of hay from the barn and dragged it out to the feeders and threw a few flakes in each. Once the herd had disengaged from round pen that still held Jelly and Chaaco, Rider dropped a few flakes on the other side of one of the sheds and led Jelly and Chaaco to their spots.

Once the horses settled into their unexpected treats of alfalfa, Rider climbed the stairs to his two room bungalow above the barn accompanied by the pups that also hadn't been in the place for six months either. Rider checked around and under the sparsely furnished abode for snakes, spiders and scorpions. He sprayed the place anyway even though he hadn't found any nasties. The plumbing and electricity still worked and he grabbed a glass and a half full bottle of whiskey and opened the door to the small deck that overlooked the Snake River and the road 500' below. Squally John was already asleep on the bed as Rider poured himself a glass of whiskey, grabbed a chair and looked down river at the ghost town of Almota, only to wonder if life would ever change back in Cloverdale.

44.

After

Rider stayed on Rattlesnake Breaks Ranch for four years after his return, and dabbled in a number of avocations that essentially kept him out in the country and away from towns. Jelly and Chaaco retired to a very happy life of range freedom. Jelly remains one of the most sought after 'rides' for Rider's neighbors and friends and truly enjoys carting around humans of various riding skills-much to his amusement. Chaaco never accepted a saddle again from anyone but Rider.

As time passed Rider began to feel his bones wither a little more every time he sat a horse, which was almost daily, and as the pain increased the scent of seaweed from his youth slowly increased. The scent of the ocean returned from some dormant tide long since drained in his soul. The fascination with ghost towns soon morphed into shipwrecks, sunken ghost towns in effect.

Through a series of events too convoluted to accurately describe, the following year Rider found himself aboard a small research vessel off the coast of rebel infested Mindanao in the Philippines hunting underwater ghost towns, and that is where we'll visit with Rider again.

The smell of seaweed had finally trumped the smell of horseshit.

About the Illustrator.

John Knight lives in York, Maine near a small fishing community called
Perkins Cove where his father's lobster boat has been moored for over
30 years. He is a graduate of the University of Maine where he majored
in biology and minored in art. He met his wife Tessa while working for
an outdoor Christian Ministry called Lifelines.   John, Tessa and their
Labrador pup 'Gus' are Owner/Operators of Four Mile Lobster Café in
Cape Neddick, adjoining his mother's Quilt shop. Both are certified
Wilderness First Responders and enjoy everything outdoors, painting,
and growing the family company Knight Underwater Bearings. You can
find more of John's artwork at *www.mainefreelanceart.com*

$15.00

ISBN 978-0-615-87480-7

51500>

9 780615 874807